POVERTY
the facts

F

3

c
a

CPAG Ltd, 1-5 Bath Street, London EC1V 9PY

CPAG promotes action for the relief, directly or indirectly, of poverty among children and families with children. We work to ensure that those on low incomes get their full entitlements to welfare benefits. In our campaigning and information work we seek to improve benefits and policies for low income families, in order to eradicate the injustice of poverty. If you are not already supporting us, please consider a donation, or ask for details of our membership schemes and publications.

Poverty Publication 93

Child Poverty Action Group
1-5 Bath Street, London EC1V 9PY

© CPAG Ltd 1996

ISBN 0 946744 49 1

Cover and design by Devious Designs 0114 275 5634
Typeset by Nancy White 0171 607 4510
Printed by Progressive Printing UK Ltd 01702 520050

CONTENTS

ACKNOWLEDGEMENTS

We are very grateful to all the people who contributed to this book. Special thanks to Fran Bennett, David Piachaud and Sally Witcher for their very valuable comments on the manuscript. Our thanks go to Lindsay Brook, Mary Carter, Katherine Duffy, Alissa Goodman and Nina Oldfield, and Margaret Frosztega, Simon Lee and Bill Scott at the DSS who helped with particular chapters. Thanks too to Jo McCrea, Peter Metcalfe, Liza Vizard and Barney Wyld at the House of Commons. Of course, the production of this, the third edition of *Poverty: the facts*, would not have been possible without the work of those who contributed to the first two editions.

Our thanks to Frances Ellery for patiently editing and managing the production of the book; Nancy White for updating and typesetting the text; Nigel Taylor for the cover design and graphics; and Peter Ridpath for promoting the book.

Finally, many thanks to colleagues at CPAG and South Bank University and our respective families for their support.

Crown copyright is reproduced with the permission of the Controller of HMSO.

FOREWORD

It is now 30 years since the birth of the Child Poverty Action Group (CPAG). During that time, we have witnessed great changes to working patterns, family structures and the social security system. Recessions have waxed and waned, often leaving permanent damage to individuals, communities and industries in their wake. Ironically, so too did the boom of the 1980s, during which poverty increased and the trend towards a reduction in inequality was decisively reversed.

Throughout, CPAG has fought to raise awareness of the extent, nature and impact of child poverty. Regrettably, the need to do so has increased over the last 30 years, as, inexcusably, has child poverty. We continue to argue that the poverty devastating the life chances of children today will have future repercussions for all. It is not good enough to dismiss children and their poverty as the private responsibility of parents. A wider social responsibility is essential if we are to ensure children are adequately supported and enable parents to provide support.

In this the third issue of *Poverty: the facts*, the key component parts of the poverty picture are explored. The facts speak for themselves – as do people in poverty who are quoted alongside. Together, they vividly describe poverty and inequality as they are in the 1990s – how they particularly impact on certain groups; the geographical dimension to the poverty map; and the housing and health implications of prolonged poverty.

Nonetheless, it would be wrong to assume that the facts will always be believed, or even that they should be accepted unchallenged: CPAG certainly examines them critically, as we would expect others to. Yet this does not justify the extent to which issues clearly revealed by research evidence are ignored by policy-makers (perhaps because it is easier to quibble about methodology than it is to address the problem exposed). Given the complexity of poverty, each approach to it can only tell part of the story. But it is striking that, whichever you select, it is clearly part of the same story, leading to the same conclusion.

˙In the 1990s, curiously, the refusal to admit the existence of poverty has been accompanied by increasing attempts to apportion blame for poverty (it is unclear how politicians and others contrive to ascribe blame for something they deny the existence of). The 'deserving' and 'undeserving' poor have long been the subject of debate – but rarely have the ranks of the 'deserving' been so depleted. As the concept of an underclass gains currency, the danger is that to be poor will be seen, *de facto*, as being undeserving. This is to deny the very real barriers to work and participation which exist for people in poverty. Yet to suggest that poverty is evidence of structural rather than personal failing is to swim against the modern-day tide of individualism.

It is not just 'the poor' and low paid who have been subject to new insecurities. Middle income professionals increasingly find themselves on short-term contracts. The downsizing and delayering of companies have confirmed to middle managers what low-paid workers have long known to be the case – that no job is for life. The negative equity trap provoked by the collapse of the housing market constitutes a new variety of poverty trap which extends way up the income distribution. Furthermore, the new restriction to mortgage interest payments, along with income support and other benefit cuts in the form of incapacity benefit and jobseeker's allowance will all impact on ex-middle Englanders who find themselves on the sharp end of the free market.

Another notable development over the last three years is the gathering cross-party obsession with tax cuts. The concept of the redistribution of income has become immensely unfashionable – or has it? Chapter 9 of *Poverty: the facts* shows that a massive transfer of income has indeed taken place – from poor to rich. Where there have been tax changes, these have fallen unevenly and, of all groups, it is families with children who have been worst hit. Overall, the lack of coherence and even blatant contradictions in policies for families with children is implicit throughout this publication.

The acute effects of the early 1990s recession may be fading, but it has left poverty and inequality trends still further entrenched. Coupled with the recent raft of social security cuts, the prospect of decreasing poverty and inequality seems remote. However, there is some cause for hope – we have seen a number of reports stressing the importance of tackling poverty and inequality from, among others, the Joseph Rowntree Foundation's *Inquiry into Income and Wealth*[1] and the Commission on Social Justice.[2]

The three years since the second edition of *Poverty: the facts* have been tremendously busy for CPAG and there is nothing to suggest that the next three will be any less so. There is no reason – except an absence of political will – why, by the year 2000, we should not be able to report that both the numbers living in poverty and the depth of their poverty have decreased. But that would still not be enough. CPAG wants more for children than survival. They need access to opportunities – to education to reach their full potential, to proper healthcare and safe places to play. Most crucially, they and their families need sufficient income to allow them to participate in the normal, everyday activities that others take for granted.

Without raising awareness, without the facts, there is little chance we will achieve our goal for children, even by CPAG's 60th birthday. We hope that *Poverty: the facts* will provide necessary ammunition to help bring about the positive and significant change so urgently needed.

Sally Witcher
Director
Child Poverty Action Group

NOTES

1. *Inquiry into Income and Wealth, Volumes 1 and 2,* Joseph Rowntree Foundation, 1995.
2. *Social Justice: strategies for national renewal,* the report of the Commission on Social Justice, Vintage, 1994.

Introduction

There is a young woman with children, suffering variously from ear-ache, asthma and hyperactivity, who explains that she is homeless because she defaulted on her mortgage. She had gone to court and agreed to make weekly payments but every time she put money aside, she found she had to borrow from it to pay for nappies and children's clothes. Told that the bailiffs were coming, she offered to make smaller weekly payments, but the building society refused, and so she fled. Now she is waiting to hear whether the council will help her or whether they will rule that she is intentionally homeless. Dr Dowson fears she will fail their test.

(N Davies, *Guardian*, 19 July 1995)[1]

Poverty is sometimes obvious – whether it is the poverty of beggars in the street, young homeless people bedded down for the night under the arches, or people rummaging in rubbish bins. At other times it is hidden inside homes, workplaces and institutions. It is not just a feature of the North or of inner cities, but widespread throughout affluent and rural areas. In 1992/93, the latest figures show that between 13 and 14 million people – around a quarter of the population in the United Kingdom – were living in poverty measured by either of the two most common definitions.[2] In 1979, less than half that number were living in poverty (defined as living below half average income after housing costs).

In the last decade and a half, the living standards of the poor and affluent have marched in opposite directions. Between 1979 and 1992/93 the real incomes (after housing costs) of those in the poorest tenth fell by 18 per cent; the average rose by 37 per cent, while the richest enjoyed a staggering rise of 61 per cent.[3] In international terms, the UK experienced the sharpest rise in inequality, with the exception of New Zealand, according to the Joseph Rowntree Foundation *Inquiry into Income and Wealth*.[4]

These figures tell the story of the 1980s and 1990s. The image of the 1980s, despite the recession of the early years, was one of growth, economic confidence and sparkling affluence. The existence, let alone the growth, of poverty was denied. But the boom proved to be ephemeral. The 1990s tell a different story. The effects of the second recession since 1979 were and continue to be felt in corners of the UK which had been untouched by the earlier recession. The continued high levels of mortgage repossessions and arrears bear witness to this. The persistence of unemployment and changes in working conditions have engendered a pervasive sense of insecurity. In *The State We're In*, Will Hutton describes a 30 per cent, 40 per cent, 40 per cent society where the bottom 30 per cent are disadvantaged, the middle 40 per cent are marginalised and insecure and the top 40 per cent are privileged.[5] The 1993 *British Social Attitudes Survey* found that four times as many people ranked job security above increased pay, a significant rise since 1989.[6]

WHY HAVE POVERTY AND INEQUALITY INCREASED SO RAPIDLY?

First, unemployment has more than doubled since 1979. At the start of 1996 it stands at well over two million, two-fifths of whom are unemployed for more than a year. At the height of the recessions it stood at around three million. But this figure hides the growing body of people who don't count as officially unemployed: people who are not available for or actively seeking work, such as lone parents and sick and disabled people, and people who have retired early. The entrenchment of unemployment, broadly defined, is a central cause of poverty and inequality. The fear of unemployment, and with it insecurity, poverty and demoralisation, hangs over many. But despite the spread of unemployment to new areas and new occupations, unemployment does not occur at random – it is shaped by class, occupation, race and gender. A construction worker is ten times more likely to be made redundant than a lawyer.

Manufacturing industry continues to contract. Many inner cities have been emptied of their old industries and crafts. Large-scale redundancies have brought poverty in their wake: associated industries close down and small shopkeepers shut up shop when people cut their spending. Alongside these long-term changes are new sources of unemployment: the construction industry has all but ground to a halt because of the stagnant housing market, local authorities have implemented redundancies and service industries are also shedding labour, with the result that there are too few new jobs to mop up those abandoned by the old industries.

Secondly, the nature of employment itself has changed radically. The industrial transformation which brought such stubbornly high levels of unemployment has reshaped the labour market. There has been a dramatic increase in the gap between the low paid and the high paid since 1978. The Rowntree report documents how the wages of the lowest paid workers born in 1950 and 1960 are static over their lifetimes and even lower than those of earlier generations.[7]

The widening gulf in earnings is the result of a complex number of factors: globalisation of the market, technological change, differences in education and experience, the decline of trade unions and government policies, such as the abolition of the Wages Councils.[8] Alongside these trends, there has been a growing divide between the so-called 'work rich' and the 'work poor' according to work by Ed Balls and Paul Gregg.[9] New work opportunities, primarily in part-time jobs have been taken up by women in married couples with a partner already in employment. Lone parents and unemployed couples have found it very difficult to take up such jobs, in part because of disincentives within the means-tested parts of the social security system. Part-time work and self-employment are frequently associated with low pay, poor working conditions and few employment and social security rights. This has a particularly serious implication for women, who make up the majority of part-time employees.

It is harder to capture the reality of poverty in work – long hours, cramped working conditions, juggling two jobs, coping with working and looking after children and meagre rates of pay. Recent research shows how the quality of work – for instance, the variety of skill, control, autonomy and job satisfaction – has important health outcomes.[10] For many, poverty is about grappling with the insecurities and frustrations associated with spells of unemployment interspersed with low-paid work. Such work patterns taint the present with poverty and offer no respite for the future.

Thirdly, these profound economic changes have gone hand in hand with shifts in family patterns. In 1991, 20 per cent of all families with children were lone parents – a rise from 8 per cent in 1971.[11] Nine out of ten lone parents are women; three-quarters of lone parents are reliant on income support. Frequently trapped by the combination of low wages and the difficulty of finding childcare, many lone mothers face a bleak future reliant on inadequate benefits.

Fourthly, the tax and social systems are seen, in Will Hutton's words, 'not as instruments of social cohesion and public purpose, rather as burdens in the fight for competitiveness'.[12] The changes in taxation since 1979 have shunted the tax burden from the affluent (in particular the very rich) to the middle and poorer groups. The roller-coaster of social security changes has been unstoppable. The Social Security Act 1986, billed as the most radical overhaul of social security since Beveridge, in contrast to its aims, failed to meet 'genuine need' and largely 'churned' the incomes of the poorest.[13] The Secretary of State for Social Security, Peter Lilley, despite his sector-by-sector approach, has severely pruned the social security budget as part of the overall review of public spending. In combination, many of the reforms have swallowed up rights and decreased benefits for some of the poorest and weakened social protection still further. Despite the squeezing of benefits, the budget has increased relentlessly as social security picks up *some* of the costs of social and economic policies and changes such as unemployment, low wages and the deregulation of the housing market. Above all, the social security system has become an increasingly inadequate tool to deal with today's problems. Designed for a full-time male workforce, it discriminates against those who have been low paid or unemployed, against those who have worked part time and people who have come to this country from abroad.

The official denial of poverty which was such a prominent feature of the 1980s is now largely discredited. For a country which has experienced two recessions, it is harder to write off the experience of millions. However, poverty is still seen by many as the fault of the poor; there is growing emphasis in the language of poverty and social security policies themselves on individual responsibility for poverty rather than on broader social factors. But, as the pages which follow demonstrate, the facts about poverty speak for themselves and the causes of poverty are primarily social rather than personal.

THE IMPACT OF POVERTY

Poverty means going short materially, socially and emotionally. It means spending less on food, on heating, and on clothing than someone on an average income. However, it is not what is spent that matters, but what isn't. Poverty means staying at home, often being bored, not seeing friends, not going to the cinema, not going out for a drink and not being able to take the children out for a trip or a treat or a holiday. It means coping with the stresses of managing on very little money, often for months or even years. It means having to withstand the onslaught of society's pressure to consume. It impinges on relationships with others and with yourself. Above all, poverty takes away the tools to create the building blocks for the future – your 'life chances'. It steals away the opportunity to have a life unmarked by sickness, a decent education, a secure home and a long retirement. It stops people being able to plan ahead. It stops people being able to take control of their lives.

So poverty widens the gap between reality and potential. But despite poverty, people struggle to make do and survive with strength, resilience and dignity in the face of immense difficulties.

PROSPECTS

The debate about how to create an inclusive society in the face of these immense changes is starting to emerge. The Joseph Rowntree Foundation's *Inquiry into Income and Wealth*,[14] the Commission on Social Justice[15] and the Dahrendorf[16] reports have firmly rejected the 'trickle down theory', that inequalities will bring greater wealth to all. Instead, in their different ways, they highlight the economic and social costs of inequality and propose policies which would begin to address these. Together with the work of others, they are part of a changing climate which recognises society's responsibility to tackle poverty and inequality on economic, social and moral grounds.

In *Poverty: the facts* we can only touch on some of these issues, yet the themes we explore lie at the heart of CPAG's work. CPAG fights for a society free from poverty. Part of our role is to act as both witness and reporter, to explain the causes of poverty and to portray poverty to a wider audience. Equipped with the facts we can argue for a society which puts an end to the exclusion of millions from society; we can argue for a society which recognises the right of all to an adequate income from employment or benefit, allowing people to participate in society as full members.

This book is intended to guide the reader to the most important facts and figures about poverty in the UK today. It does not attempt to explain in detail the range of possible solutions to poverty. It looks at official and independent data on poverty and low incomes, the causes of poverty, different dimensions of deprivation, the experience of women and Black and minority ethnic groups, disparities between the countries and regions of the UK, how the UK compares to the rest of Europe, and growing inequalities. In doing so, it draws on the work of researchers, academics and government statisticians, as well as the views of ordinary people.

NOTES

1. N Davies, 'Shoved through the social safety net', *Guardian*, 19 July 1995.
2. DSS, *Households below Average Income 1979–1992/93, a statistical analysis and revised figures*, HMSO, 1995; and Social Security Committee, *Second Report, Low Income Statistics: Low Income Families, 1989–1992*, HMSO, 1995.
3. DSS, *Households below Average Income*, see note 2.
4. *Inquiry into Income and Wealth, Volumes 1 and 2*, Joseph Rowntree Foundation, 1995.
5. W Hutton, *The State We're In*, Jonathan Cape, 1995.
6. R Jowell, J Curtice, L Brook and D Ahrendt (eds), *British Social Attitudes, the 11th report*, SCPR, Dartmouth, 1994.
7. See note 4.
8. See note 4.
9. E Balls and P Gregg, *Work and Welfare: tackling the jobs deficit*, Institute for Public Policy, 1995.
10. B Graetz, 'Health consequences of employment and unemployment: longitudinal evidence for young men and women', *Social Science Medicine*, Vol 35, No 6, 1993; and M G Marmot *et al*, 'Health Inequalities among British Civil Servants: the Whitehall II Study', *Lancet*, Vol 337, pp1387-93, 1991.
11. J Haskey, 'Estimated numbers of one-parent families and their prevalence in Great Britain in 1991', *Population Trends 78*, pp5–19, 1994.
12. See note 5.
13. M Evans, D Piachaud and H Sutherland, *Designed for the Poor – Poorer by Design? The effects of the 1986 Social Security Act on family incomes*, STICERD, WSP/105, 1994.
14. See note 4.
15. *Social Justice, Strategies for National Renewal*, the report of the Commission on Social Justice, Vintage, 1994.
16. R Dahrendorf *et al*, *Report on Wealth Creation and Social Cohesion in a Free Society*, The Commission on Wealth Creation and Social Cohesion, 1995.

Definitions and debates

DEFINITIONS: WHAT IS POVERTY?

Poverty is not only about shortage of money. It is about rights and relationships; about how people are treated and how they regard themselves; about powerlessness, exclusion and loss of dignity. Yet the lack of an adequate income is at its heart.

(*Faith in the City*)[1]

Homeless people sleeping under the arches, pensioners counting out the pennies in the supermarket. A family crowded into a single room in a bed and breakfast hotel, mothers stretching out child benefit until their next giro comes. The fear of the debt collector, the queues for a housing transfer, for benefit, for advice … there is no doubt that these are the manifestations of poverty. However, in other respects poverty is difficult to define. For example, how does poverty in Britain compare to poverty in India? How is the perception of poverty modified from one generation to the next? Is poverty for one family the same as poverty for another? Is poverty experienced in the same way by men and women? British governments of all political persuasions have refused to define an *official* 'poverty line'. As a consequence, there is no official yardstick for measuring the rise or fall in poverty under different governments. This said, we can identify broad approaches to defining poverty.

ABSOLUTE POVERTY

An *absolute* definition of poverty assumes that it is possible to define a minimum standard of living based on a person's *biological* needs for food, water, clothing and shelter. The emphasis is on basic physical needs and not on broader social and cultural needs. Absolute poverty is when people fall below this level – when they cannot house, clothe or feed themselves.

Seebohm Rowntree used such a definition in his study of poverty in York in 1899. He devised a 'primary' poverty line based on a standard of minimum needs for food, clothing, heating and rent, to show that many families had incomes below this level. But, as he himself wrote:[2]

> My primary poverty line represented the minimum sum on which physical efficiency could be maintained. It was a bare standard of subsistence rather than living ... such a minimum does not by any means constitute a reasonable living wage.

The absolute view of poverty has been adopted by various policy makers and influential organisations, such as the World Bank.[3] While evidence of large-scale starvation and destitution in less-developed countries strengthen the perception of what constitutes 'absolute' poverty, this concept of poverty has also been used to suggest that poverty no longer exists in the UK. In 1976, former Secretary of State for Social Services, Lord Joseph, argued:[4]

> An absolute standard of means is defined by reference to the actual needs of the poor and not by reference to the expenditure of those who are not poor. A family is poor if it cannot afford to eat ... By any absolute standards there is very little poverty in Britain today.

John Moore, Secretary of State for Social Security, perpetuated this view in 1989 when he claimed that economic success had put an end to absolute poverty. The debate has continued, however, and was more recently revived by comments from the Duke of Edinburgh.[5]

This tougher definition of poverty is the one which appears to be shared by the general public. In 1990 the British Social Attitudes Survey found that 60 per cent of people agreed that poverty was about subsistence; 95 per cent agreed that poverty was about living below minimum subsistence; and only 25 per cent thought that poverty was relative to the living standards of others.[6] The appeal of an absolute definition of poverty is its apparent clarity and its moral force. Put simply, someone is poor if he or she does not have enough to eat.

However, the absolute definition is flawed, for two main reasons. First, it is very difficult to define an 'adequate' minimum when standards of living themselves change over time. Beveridge recognised this in *Social Insurance and Allied Services* in 1942:

> determination of what is required for reasonable human subsistence is to some extent a matter of judgement; estimates on this point change with time, and generally in a progressive community, change upwards.[7]

How we house, clothe and feed ourselves has changed drastically over the years. Living standards also vary radically in different cultures. People's expectations also change because of the demands society makes of them, so that a minimum standard of living is shaped by the way society as a whole behaves and spends its money. Thus, an adequate minimum is itself defined by what is socially acceptable. Secondly, an absolute definition takes no account of social and cultural needs.

Such considerations demand a more sophisticated approach to the definition of poverty.

RELATIVE POVERTY

> One of the most draining and debilitating aspects of poverty in the UK or USA is that the poor person lives in a rich society where people are valued according to what they own....where a whole people suffer, poverty does not point the finger of failure at the individual as poignantly and mercilessly as where poverty comes in the midst of affluence.[8]

In this instance poverty is defined in relation to a generally accepted standard of living in a specific society at a particular time and goes beyond basic biological needs. This view of poverty has a long heritage. Adam Smith, the eighteenth-century economic philosopher, commented:

> By necessities I understand not only commodities which are indispensably necessary for the support of life but whatever *the custom of the country* renders it indecent for creditable people, even of the lowest order, to be without.
>
> (Adam Smith, *The Wealth of Nations*, our emphasis)[9]

In 1979, Peter Townsend's definitive work, *Poverty in the UK*, provided a forceful presentation of a relative view of poverty which echoed Smith's concerns:

Individuals ... can be said to be in poverty when they lack the resources to obtain the types of diet, participate in the activities and have the living conditions and amenities which are customary, or at least widely encouraged or approved, in the societies to which they belong.[10]

Thus poverty is not simply about lack of money but also about exclusion from the customs of society. While there are a number of difficulties inherent in this approach – for example, how do we establish what the norms of our society are, or what people *choose* to manage without? – such a perspective has played a crucial role in establishing a new agenda for contemporary debates about poverty.[11]

The relative view of poverty has been shared by people across the political spectrum. For example, when she was a Conservative social security minister, Lady Chalker said:

It is not sufficient to assess poverty by absolute standards; nowadays it must be judged on relative criteria by comparison with the standard of living of other groups in the community ... beneficiaries must have an income which enables them to participate in the life of the community.[12]

More recently, Alan Howarth, former Conservative minister for education and science, has put forward a relative view of poverty:

I put it to my hon. Friends that they should not insist that only absolute poverty matters. Relative poverty matters very much indeed because we define ourselves as members of society.[13]

Relative poverty is about social exclusion imposed by an inadequate income. It is not only about having to go short of food or clothing in the UK in the 1990s; it is also about not being able to join a local sports club, or send your children on a school trip, or go out with friends, or have a Christmas dinner:

I hated Christmas, I would have preferred it for people not to give me anything because I wouldn't have felt obliged to give back. I found it very hard ... like in November, if I found I had a pound or two spare I would put it in a jar ... I gave them all some little thing each, but you feel like it is nothing.[14]

As Jo Roll argues, a relative definition of poverty encompasses the view that:

It is not just that the physical needs have a social aspect but that social needs should be recognised in their own right.[15]

In a development of the relative approach, Joanna Mack and Stewart Lansley adopted an innovative approach to poverty which has been described as consensual or democratic.[16] They defined being in poverty as a situation in which people had to live without the things which society as a whole regarded as necessities. Using public opinion surveys, they found that there was general agreement about what constituted a minimum standard of living. At least two out of three people thought the following were necessities in 1990:

- self-contained damp-free accommodation with an indoor toilet and bath;
- three daily meals for each child and two meals a day for adults;
- adequate bedrooms and beds;
- heating and carpeting;
- a refrigerator and washing machine;
- enough money for special occasions like Christmas;
- toys for the children.

In 1990, they found that around 11 million people – one in five of the population – lacked three of these necessities or more, which they defined as living in poverty.[17]

In CPAG's publication, *Family Fortunes*, the authors adopted a similar approach to defining and measuring poverty by asking parents to draw up a minimum budget, based on consensus achieved through group discussion, reflecting the minimum needed for bringing up a child in the 1990s.[18]

CPAG has always supported the view that poverty should be seen in relation to the standard of living in a particular society. People should have a right to an income which allows them to participate in society, rather than merely exist. Such participation involves having the means to fulfil responsibilities to others such as partners, sons and daughters, to care for elderly or sick relatives, to help neighbours and friends, and to be able to join in as workers and citizens.

A relative definition of poverty is not without its problems, however. As Jo Roll has argued:

A definition of poverty which is entirely relative to a particular society has a number of problems, even for those who recognise the social aspects of poverty. In particular, if no other standard is applied, a relative definition would deny the existence of poverty in a country where everyone was starving and if everybody's living standards fell drastically but evenly, the numbers of poor people would not change.[19]

Amartya Sen has also challenged the relative definition of poverty by suggesting that such a definition should not overlook the fact that 'there is an irreducible absolutist core in the idea of poverty'.[20] Sen defines absolute poverty in terms of fixed measures (eg, nutritional requirements, to be sheltered, to be clothed, to be able to travel, etc) rather than in relation to living standards of others in society. This translates into a similar method, adopted by Peter Townsend and others, whereby fixed measures are used to measure relative living standards.[21]

This underlines how much of the debate about defining poverty is about semantics – a focus which at times threatens to obscure the very fact that poverty *exists* and that there is a need to act to address this. As Jo Roll has observed:[22]

> Although it might be possible to use the word 'poor' in a neutral sense simply to mean a lack or shortage of something, this is not the meaning which has caused so much controversy. 'Poverty' is widely used to describe situations which are unacceptable and about which something needs to be done.

DEBATES: THE POVERTY CONTROVERSY

POVERTY: A DISAPPEARING TERM?

Poverty is a term which is rarely heard on the lips of policy makers. The word 'poor' was once described by a senior Civil Servant as 'one that the Government actually disputes'.[23] When, in 1989, John Moore, the then Secretary of State for Social Security, claimed that economic success had put an end to *absolute* poverty and that *relative* poverty simply meant inequality, there was a storm of protest. The speech touched a raw nerve – whatever facts and figures were produced to justify the claims of the 'end of poverty', there was no doubt in the minds of both the people living in poverty and those who witnessed it at close quarters that nothing could be further from the truth.

But policy makers have not reclaimed the word poverty. Despite evidence that there is concern about the impact of rising levels of poverty, as evidenced by a leaked memo from senior civil servants,[24] there has been no public airing of such concern. The debate since the late 1980s has been characterised by bland euphemisms – 'low income', 'below average income', 'the bottom ten per cent' – terms which obscure the reality of deprivation, poverty and hardship.

While it is true that some people living in poverty do not wish to be identified as 'poor', if the word 'poverty' is obliterated from public discussion, the experience of people in poverty disappears from our perception of social reality.

Words which have a heavy negative resonance have been far more prominent in debates about living standards in the 1990s. In particular, the emphasis of debates has frequently been on the responsibility which individuals have for their own circumstances. While individual behaviour clearly has some role, it cannot be the predominant explanation for the rapid increase in poverty in recent decades. Nevertheless, attention has been diverted away from the need for government action to reduce poverty towards a moralistic debate about individual responsibility.

DEPENDENCY

Poverty is increasingly being defined in terms of dependency. 'Welfare dependency' has been a central concern of policy makers, particularly since the constraints on welfare spending following the oil crisis of the mid-1970s and the election in 1979 of a government committed to a programme of reducing state intervention.[25] The term now is in widespread use among policy makers and the media to refer to individuals' long-term reliance on social security benefits. Increasingly, the term has had a built-in inference as to the cause of that dependency – placing the blame on the individuals themselves.

There have been increasing references from policy makers of differing political persuasions to individuals' responsibility for their own circumstances, an emphasis which overshadows discussion about the need for collective action for those who are most in need of support.

> I will tell you who attack duty and responsibility. Those politicians who claim the state is responsible for everything and everyone ... Those who believe the welfare state should cope with everything.[26]

This view has been reflected in policy changes. Increasing emphasis has been placed on the behaviour of unemployed claimants rather than on the need for government to take action on creating jobs. For example, the new jobseeker's allowance reinforces the 'link between looking for work and receiving benefit'[27] by obliging claimants to sign a jobseeker's agreement. The jobseeker's allowance White Paper acknowledged that the jobseeker's allowance will 'bring a new focus on the experience and actions of unemployed people as individuals' and that 'it will emphasise the responsibilities of unemployed people to take effective steps to secure a job.'

Gordon Brown, the Shadow Chancellor, has argued:

> Simply remaining unemployed and permanently on benefits will no longer be an option. If we do not act, a generation of young people will have been abandoned, with social division, crime, alienation, and all the consequent problems for the next 40 years.[28]

Despite a difference of emphasis, the Labour Party has sometimes adopted the term 'welfare dependency' and has called for the elimination of 'the social evil of welfare dependency among able-bodied people'.[29] Welfare dependency is increasingly associated in debates with many of society's problems, reinforcing its negative resonance.

Much of the commentary on welfare dependency has focused on lone parents. The rapid increase in the proportion of lone parents living on income support – from 38 per cent in 1979 to 73 per cent in 1992 – has prompted some commentators to note that, in Frank Field's words:

> Single mothers [are] the main cause of poverty or welfare dependency amongst children.[30]

Such statements emphasise the link between poverty and lone parent-hood *per se* rather than the circumstances which arise from lone parenthood (difficulty juggling childcare, the impact of the poverty trap, etc). On the Right the availability of welfare benefits is seen as encouraging lone parenthood (and unemployment), and thus poverty; James Bartholomew, writing in the *Daily Telegraph*, argues:

> If one looks at it from a purely financial point of view, we pay people to be unemployed and we pay them extra if they are lone parents. We should not really be surprised that the result has been mass unemployment and a seven-fold rise in the number of lone parents. We have encouraged these things. We have removed the natural disincentive to lone parenthood. We can only solve the problems by putting them back in place.[31]

Such concerns have prompted proposals to cut welfare benefits for lone parents and restrict their access to council housing.[32]

There are several objections to the way in which the notion of 'dependency' is being used in debates about poverty. First, many claimants do not want to rely on state benefits but have little choice because of few employment or training opportunities, the poverty trap and inadequate childcare facilities. Their dependency is therefore not self-inflicted as the use of the term implies.

Secondly, the stigmatisation of dependency is extremely limited – it focuses solely on social security benefits and on certain groups of claimants; the same commentary is not made with reference to pensioners, for example. Neither is reliance on tax reliefs or allowances seen as dependency.

Thirdly, policies which aim to reduce dependence on certain kinds of state support often push people into greater dependence on families, friends, relatives and charity or leave them without support at all. Dependency does not vanish with the erosion of support from the state, but simply finds a new focus.

Finally, it is absurd to consider independence and dependence as anything other than in relative terms. We are all dependent on state support – some of us for life, others at particular times and in specific circumstances.

THE 'UNDERCLASS'

> I see the growth of a so-called underclass as the most formidable challenge to a secure and civilised way of life throughout the developed world. Our society cannot afford to alienate and exclude significant numbers of the poor, the black and the young.
>
> (Rt Hon Kenneth Clarke QC MP)[33]

The term 'underclass' has proved to be of enduring use. A broad cross-section of leader writers, academics and journalists seem to hold the belief that Britain is characterised by the growth of an 'underclass' which is cut off from the rest of society.[34] This so-called underclass has been described by a variety of groups and individuals as the root cause of a plethora of problems, such as declining education standards, social unrest and crime.

There are broadly two approaches to the 'underclass' debate. One approach, which is usually, though not entirely, associated with the political right, sees the underclass primarily as a 'cultural' phenomenon. The other approach, associated more with the left, sees the 'underclass' as a structural phenomenon, the result of social and economic changes.[35]

Chief among those who see the 'underclass' as a cultural

phenomenon is American political scientist Charles Murray.[36] In an article in the *Sunday Times*, Murray defined the characteristics of the 'underclass': high rates of illegitimacy, of crime and of drop-out from the labour market.[37] Thus the term 'underclass' describes a type of poverty that is defined by behaviour:

> When I use the term 'underclass' I am indeed focusing on a certain type of poor person defined not by his condition – eg, long-term unemployed – but by his *deplorable behaviour in response to that condition* – eg, unwilling to take the jobs that are available to him.[38] (our emphasis)

From the point of view of their exponents, both 'dependency' and 'underclass' appeal because they create a distinction between different groups of people in poverty. A new lease of life is given to the old distinction between the deserving and undeserving poor.

In the United States, discussion of the 'underclass' is dominated by the issue of 'race'. Murray's *The Bell Curve*[39] has added to the 'underclass' debate by arguing that there is a direct link between 'race' and intelligence. In the UK, the issue of 'race' is not so prevalent in debates about the 'underclass'. This does not reflect racial tolerance but a less explicit approach to 'race' issues in the UK.

For Murray and others, the solution to the problem of the 'underclass' is not money, or training, or education. Instead, they suggest that the answer lies in a radical dose of 'self-government', whereby the views of local communities determine welfare policy. Digby Anderson presents the case rather more starkly than most by arguing for the return of social stigma and other disincentives in order to 'dissuade people from poverty-producing behaviour.'[40]

By contrast, other commentators have used the term in a quite different way. For example, Garry Runciman places the 'underclass' in his overall schema of social classes:

> That there is below the two working classes an underclass which constitutes a separate category of roles is ... readily demonstrable ... But the term must be understood to stand not for a group or category of workers systematically disadvantaged within the labour market ... but for those members of British society whose roles place them more or less permanently at the economic level where benefits are paid by the state to those unable to participate in the labour market at all.[41]

Frank Field adopts a similar approach.[42] For Field, the creation of such a class is primarily the consequence of structural factors and in his definition comprises the long-term unemployed, lone parents and those elderly people who are dependent solely on state benefits. He sees the 'underclass' as excluded from the rights of citizenship, separated from the rest of society in terms of 'income, life chances and aspirations'. He believes that, alongside other measures, policies on maintenance, pensions and availability for work will help to reduce its numbers.

Ralf Dahrendorf straddles the two approaches, seeing the 'underclass' as rooted in economic and social changes – ie, that modern societies can have satisfactory rates of growth while substantial minorities remain unemployed.[43] But he also argues that:

> the underclass is the living doubt in the prevailing values which will eat into the texture of the societies in which we are living. In fact, it has already done so, which is why there is a very strong moral case for doing something about it.[44]

So how useful is the term 'underclass'? Arguably its key strength is that it is an attempt to capture an intensity of poverty. It conveys the ways in which different aspects of poverty such as low quality housing, a bleak urban environment, social isolation, exclusion from the world of paid work and lack of participation in political life compound one another.

However, despite this advantage there are several objections to using the term. First, it is imprecise. Murray has used it to describe behaviour. Others, such as Frank Field, have placed the 'underclass' in the context of social and economic trends. It is not clear whether the 'underclass' describes all the poor, or subgroups of the poor. Why are large groups of the poor, such as pensioners, often not included? If the term only refers to subgroups, precisely which subgroups fall into this category and why? Is the underclass defined by its economic status or its 'deviance' from the norm?

Secondly, there is little empirical evidence to support the cultural interpretation of the 'underclass'. In a study of attitudes of families who had been long-term unemployed, Antony Heath found that their values and attitudes were very similar to those of the employed.[45] This is borne out by a study of people on benefit in Newcastle-upon-Tyne. In short, there is no clear evidence that such a class exists:

> At a time when British poverty is again being discussed in terms of an underclass, it is of crucial importance to recognise that these families,

and probably millions more like them living on social security benefits, are in no sense a detached and isolated group cut off from the rest of society. They are just the same people as the rest of our population, with the same culture and aspirations but with simply too little money to be able to share in the activities and possessions of everyday life with the rest of the population.

(Living on the Edge)[46]

Thirdly, the predominance of 'cultural' or 'behavioural' interpretations of the 'underclass' is profoundly worrying. It allows poverty to be explained away by personal and moral considerations, while allowing social and economic factors to be conveniently overshadowed. This is not to suggest that people's behaviour does not matter, but that poverty cannot be explained solely or mainly in terms of that behaviour.

Fourthly, the term 'underclass' is often heavy with negative resonance. It brings to mind the underworld, the sub-human, 'Hobbesian savagery',[47] the underbelly of society, the wayward, drunken, feckless, 'dangerous' classes that the Victorians inveighed against.

The underclass *spawns* illegitimate children without a care for tomorrow and *feeds* on a crime rate which rivals the United States in property offences. Its able-bodied youths see no point in working and feel no compulsion either. They reject society while *feeding* off it; they are becoming a lost generation giving the cycle of deprivation a new spin ... No amount of income redistribution or social engineering can solve their problem. Their *sub*-lifestyles are beyond welfare benefit rises and job creation schemes. They exist as active social outcasts, wedded to an anti-social system.

(Sunday Times editorial, our emphasis)[48]

The 'underclass' is described as though it were a parasite, spawning offspring and feeding off the rest of society. Thus, the term expresses more about the *fears* of the rest of society than about the reality it seeks to describe. As Ruth Lister has suggested:

The danger is that the more certain groups in poverty are described in such value-laden language, the easier it becomes for the rest of society to write them off as beyond the bonds of common citizenship.[49]

A more fruitful approach to this debate would be to focus on the ways in which poor people are excluded and marginalised by society itself; to identify the barriers to participation rather than blaming the people beyond the barriers.[50]

SOCIAL EXCLUSION

'Social exclusion' ... derives from the idea of society as a status hierarchy comprising people bound together by rights and obligations that reflect, and are defined with respect to, a shared moral order.
(Robert Walker in G Room (ed), *Beyond the Threshold*, 1995)[51]

A term which is being more widely used in Europe and by the European Commission is that of 'social exclusion' (see Chapter 8). The 1995 UN Summit for Social Development also included the need to address social exclusion among its declared priorities.

Social exclusion is not the same as poverty. As Katherine Duffy notes:

Social exclusion is a broader concept than poverty, encompassing not only low material means but the inability to participate effectively in economic, social, political and cultural life, and, in some characterisations, alienation and distance from the mainstream society.[52]

Social exclusion is defined in terms of the denial of civil, political, social, economic and cultural rights, and reflects a relative view of living standards and opportunities. Debates about social exclusion provoke discussion about the needs for policies to ensure that individuals can participate fully in society. As the *Joseph Rowntree Inquiry into Income and Wealth* argued:

Policy-makers should be concerned with the way in which the living standards of a substantial minority of the population have lagged behind since the late 1970s. Not only is this a problem for those directly affected, it also damages the social fabric and so affects us all.[53]

Social exclusion will not be overcome unless policy makers listen to the needs of those living in poverty.[54] While there will be groups which are socially excluded who may not be poor, the inclusion/exclusion dimension enriches poverty debates by going beyond a narrow definition of lack of resources. This has more far-reaching implications for policy proposals.

CONCLUSION

We have looked at different approaches to poverty and have argued that it is crucial to consider poverty in relation to the living standards of the rest of society. To do without the things that the rest of society regards as essential – a fridge, toys for the children, being able to give a birthday present – is to experience real poverty. We have looked at the poverty debate from different perspectives: dependency, the underclass and social exclusion. The pages which follow concentrate on the facts about, and the causes of, poverty. They show that, despite society's prosperity, the number of people living in poverty has increased and that this poverty is the outcome not of inadequacy but of broader social and economic factors.

NOTES

1. The report of the Archbishop of Canterbury's Commission on Urban Priority Areas, *Faith in the City, a call for action by church and nation*, Vol 15, Part 1, Church House, 1985.
2. Quoted in J Veit Wilson, 'Paradigms of poverty', *Journal of Social Policy*, January 1986.
3. K Duffy, *Social Exclusion and Human Dignity in Europe: background report for the proposed initiative by the Council of Europe*, Steering Committee on Social Policy (CDPS), Council of Europe, 1995.
4. K Joseph, *Stranded on middle ground*, Centre for Policy Studies, 1976.
5. *Independent*, 10 June 1994.
6. P Taylor-Gooby, 'Social Welfare: the unkindest cuts', in R Jowell *et al* (eds), *British Social Attitudes, the 7th Report*, Gower, 1990.
7. Sir William Beveridge, *Social Insurance and Allied Services*, Cmnd 6404, 1942, quoted in J Roll, *Understanding poverty, a guide to the concepts and measures*, Family Policy Studies Centre, 1992 .
8. R McCloughry, *The Eye of the Needle*, Inter Varsity Press, 1990, quoted in C Philo (ed), *Off the Map: the social geography of poverty in the UK*, CPAG Ltd, 1995.
9. Adam Smith, *The Wealth of Nations*, 1812.
10. P Townsend, *Poverty in the UK*, Penguin, 1979.
11. *See* debate between David Piachaud and Peter Townsend in *New Society*, 10 and 18 September 1981.
12. House of Commons, 6 November 1979.
13. House of Commons, *Hansard*, 14 February 1995, col 862.
14. Quoted in E Kempson, A Bryson and K Rowlingson, *Hard times? How poor families make ends meet*, Policy Studies Institute, 1994.
15. J Roll, *see* note 7.

16. J Mack and S Lansley, *Poor Britain*, Allen & Unwin, 1985. This work is updated in *Breadline Britain 1990s*, the findings of the television series, Domino Films, LWT, 1991.
17. *See* note 16.
18. S Middleton, K Ashworth and R Walker, *Family Fortunes: pressures on parents and children in the 1990s*, CPAG Ltd, 1994.
19. *See* note 7.
20. A Sen, *Poor, relatively speaking*, Oxford Economic Papers, 25, pp135-169, 1983.
21. D Gordon and C Pantazia (eds), *Breadline Britain in the 1990s: a report to the Joseph Rowntree Foundation*, Department of Social Policy and Planning, University of Bristol, 1995.
22. *See* note 7.
23. Assistant Secretary for policy on family benefits and low incomes, DHSS, evidence to the Select Committee on Social Services, 15 June 1988, quoted in D Gordon and C Pantazia (eds), *see* note 21.
24. *Guardian*, 13 February 1995.
25. H Dean and P Taylor-Gooby, *Dependency Culture: the explosion of a myth*, Harvester/Wheatsheaf, 1992.
26. John Major, speech to the Conservative Central Council Meeting, Birmingham, 1 April 1995.
27. DSS and DE, *Jobseeker's White Paper*, HMSO, October 1994.
28. G Brown, 'Brown unveils back-to-work scheme', *Financial Times*, 10 November 1995.
29. Tony Blair, 'The rights we enjoy reflect the duties we owe', The Spectator Lecture, March 1995.
30. F Field, *Making Welfare Work: reconstructing welfare for the millennium*, Institute of Community Studies, 1995.
31. J Bartholomew, 'Don't take single parents for granted: stop the hand-outs', *Daily Telegraph*, 15 August 1995.
32. Chancellor of the Exchequer, Budget Statement, 28 November 1995, and Housing White Paper, *Our Future Homes*, Department of the Environment, 1995.
33. Speech by the Rt Hon Kenneth Clarke QC MP to the Tory Reform Group, 24 November 1991.
34. C Oppenheim in *Social Work Today*, 26 October 1992.
35. D Smith (ed), *Understanding the Underclass*, Policy Studies Institute, 1992.
36. The full exposition of some of Murray's views can be found in C Murray, *Losing Ground*, Basic Books Inc (USA), 1984. More recently, Murray has elaborated his views on the 'underclass' in *Underclass: the crisis deepens*, Institute for Economic Affairs, 1994.
37. *Sunday Times*, 26 November 1989.
38. C Murray, *'Rejoinder', the emerging British underclass*, Institute of Economic Affairs, 1990.

39. *See* note 25.
40. D Anderson, *Sunday Times*, 20 May 1990.
41. G Runciman, quoted in D Smith (ed), *see* note 35.
42. F Field, *Losing Out: the emergence of Britain's underclass*, Blackwell, 1989.
43. R Dahrendorf, quoted in D Smith (ed), *see* note 35.
44. *See* note 40.
45. A Heath, quoted in D Smith (ed), *see* note 35.
46. J Bradshaw and H Holmes, *Living on the Edge: a study of the living standards of families on benefit in Tyne and Wear*, Tyneside CPAG, 1989.
47. T Dalrymple, 'The underclass: nasty, brutish and short of human hope', *Daily Telegraph*, 25 January 1993.
48. *Sunday Times*, 26 November 1989.
49. R Lister, *The Exclusive Society: citizenship and the poor*, CPAG Ltd, 1990.
50. *See* P Golding (ed), *Excluding the Poor*, CPAG, 1986.
51. G Room (ed), *Beyond the Threshold, the measurement and analysis of social exclusion*, The Policy Press, 1995.
52. *See* note 3.
53. *Inquiry into Income and Wealth, Volume 1*, Joseph Rowntree Foundation, 1995.
54. *See* note 50.

2 Poverty: the facts

Measuring poverty is an exercise in demarcation. Lines have to be drawn where none may be visible and they have to be made bold. Where one draws the line is itself a battlefield.

(Meghnad Desai, *Excluding the Poor*)[1]

INTRODUCTION

CPAG is in no doubt about the existence, growth and nature of poverty in the United Kingdom today. At its heart, poverty is about exclusion from social participation. However, unlike other countries such as the United States, the United Kingdom has no official poverty line – no government-sanctioned marker which admits the existence of poverty. Nevertheless, since our task is to estimate the extent of poverty, we need to establish such a line – one which divides those who are poor from those who are not poor.

We have chosen to look at two possible poverty lines.

The first poverty line is based on the *Low Income Families* (LIF)[2] statistics which were originally published by the DSS (for the years 1972–85), subsequently by the independent Institute for Fiscal Studies and now under the auspices of the House of Commons Social Security Committee.[3] This series shows the numbers of people living on, below or just above the supplementary benefit/income support level. CPAG uses supplementary benefit/income support as a proxy for the first poverty line.

The second poverty line is based on the *Households below Average Income*[4] statistics with which the government replaced LIF. We use 50 per cent of average income after housing costs, adjusted for family size, as a proxy for the second poverty line.

Each approach has its strengths and weaknesses and by examining the two side by side we are able to present a more comprehensive picture of poverty (Appendix 1 has a full discussion of these issues).

The first approach, which uses supplementary benefit/income support as a poverty line, allows us to assess how many people are on or below what the state deems a minimum level of income for people who are not in 'full-time' work. Income support (as was its predecessor, supplementary benefit) is set each year by Parliament and is supposed to function as a 'safety net'. Thus, it is a crucial way of assessing the effectiveness of the government's own minimum income guarantee.

The second approach, which uses half of average income after housing costs as a poverty line, draws on official data and is an explicitly relative measure which looks at how people at the bottom of the income distribution have fared in relation to the average.

KEY RESULTS

As we shall see, despite their different approaches, what both methods reveal is that:

- in 1992, 4,740,000 people (8 per cent of the population) were living *below* income support level. In 1979, 6 per cent of the population were living below the supplementary benefit level;[5/6]
- in 1992, 13,680,000 people (24 per cent of the population) were living on or below the income support level. In 1979, 14 per cent of the population were living on or below the supplementary benefit level;[7]
- in 1992/93, 14.1 million people (25 per cent of the population) were living below 50 per cent of average income after housing costs. In 1979, 9 per cent of the population were living below 50 per cent of average income after housing costs.[8]

So, whichever way you measure it, poverty has grown significantly over recent years and by 1992/93, between 13 and 14 million people in the United Kingdom – around a quarter of our society – were living in poverty.

CONTEXT

What is the context in which we are looking at the changes in poverty? The figures from both series cover the period 1979 to 1992/93. During that time there were major economic and social changes. Between 1979 and 1993, such changes included:[9]

- a rise in the Gross National Product (GNP) of 27 per cent in real (ie, after inflation) terms, although the rise was not consistent over this period and real GNP fell by 2 per cent to 3 per cent between 1979 and 1981 because of the recession;
- very substantial rises in average incomes – a rise of around 41 per cent in real personal disposable income;
- average earnings rose by 34 per cent in real terms, but the earnings of the rich and poor became more dispersed;
- prices increased by 148 per cent;
- a very sharp rise in unemployment, which rose from just over 1 million to just under 3 million in 1993 and has stayed at over 2 million since;
- increases in the proportion of the population receiving means-tested benefits from 17 per cent in 1979 to 25 per cent in 1992/93;
- the weakening of some contributory parts of the social security system such as sickness and unemployment benefits, leaving many more people to fall back on means-tested benefits;
- a change in employment patterns, with the growth of part-time, temporary and self-employed work;
- bonuses for the average earner and windfalls for the rich through reductions in income tax. However, national insurance contributions and indirect taxes were increased;
- increases in the number of single adults below pension age without children, pensioners and lone parent families – all these groups tend to have lower than average incomes;
- decreases in the number of couples with children and children in general.

In short, the persistence of high unemployment coupled with increased average incomes forged a much wider gap between the people who were dependent solely on benefits (which generally rise by the level of inflation only) or reliant on low wages and those on average earnings and above.

WHAT THE FIGURES MISS OUT

Both *Low Income Families* (LIF) and *Households below Average Income* (HBAI) are derived from the same source – the *Family Expenditure Survey* (FES), an annual government survey of around 7,000 households in the UK. Due to the nature of the FES, both LIF and HBAI *exclude* the following from their figures:

- people living in institutions – eg, hospitals, nursing homes, residential homes and prisons;
- homeless people.

Neither do they provide an analysis of the data by sex or ethnic origin. The exclusion of homeless people and people living in institutions means that *all* the figures we present below are likely to be an *underestimate*. This is because homeless people and people living in institutions often have very little money.

THE FIRST SOURCE: LOW INCOME FAMILIES STATISTICS

WHAT ARE THE LOW INCOME FAMILIES STATISTICS?

The *Low Income Families* statistics 1989–1992 (LIF), produced by the Institute for Fiscal Studies (IFS), were published by the House of Commons Social Security Committee in March 1995.[10] LIF show the numbers of people living on, below and up to 140 per cent of supplementary benefit/income support. Income support replaced supplementary benefit as part of the 1988 social security changes. Like its predecessor, supplementary benefit, it is a means-tested benefit for people who are not in 'full-time' work (see Appendix 2 for full definition). However, it has a different structure from supplementary benefit. Instead of scale rates and extra weekly additions for certain needs such as heating and diet, income support consists of personal allowances and premia for certain groups such as families with children, pensioners, lone parents, disabled people and carers. This change in the social security system has created some difficulties in looking at these figures over time. However, the IFS has attempted to create a continuous series.[11]

CPAG defines all those living on and below supplementary benefit/income support as living in poverty. It also looks at those people living between 100 per cent and 140 per cent of the supplementary benefit/income support level and describes them as living on the *margins* of poverty.

WHAT IS THE POVERTY LINE IN THE LOW INCOME FAMILIES STATISTICS?

The poverty line is measured by the level of income support. It shows that in 1992/93 a two-parent family with two children below 11 years of age were living in poverty if they had an income (after paying for their housing costs) of £105 a week or less. In 1995/96 the same type of family is living in poverty if they have an income (after housing costs) of £115.15 a week. In Table 2.1 we show what the poverty line is for different families, using the income support level and below to define poverty. We chose 1992/93 as this was the year for the latest LIF statistics and 1995/96 to show what the poverty line would be today.

TABLE 2.1: **The poverty line using income support (after housing costs)**

		Income support rates
Family type	April 1992–March 1993[1]	April 1995–March 1996[1]
Non-pensioners		
Single person: aged 18-24	£33.60	£36.80
aged 25+	£42.45	£46.50
Lone parent with 1 child		
aged under 11[2]	£71.05	£77.90
Couple[3]	£66.60	£73.00
Couple with 2 children[4]		
(aged under 11)	£105.00	£115.15
Pensioners (aged 60–74)		
Single person	£57.15[5]	£65.10
Couple	£88.95[6]	£101.05

Notes:
1. These figures are the levels of benefit that were paid at the time (ie, they are cash figures which are not adjusted for inflation).
2. Lone parent is aged 18 or over.
3. At least one member of the couple is aged 18 or over.
4. See note 3.
5. This figure relates to payments between April and October 1992. After October 1992, the income support rate for single pensioners increased to £59.15.
6. This figure relates to payments between April and October 1992. After October 1992 the income support rate for couple pensioners increased to £91.95.

Source: *National Welfare Benefits Handbook* 1992/93, 1995/96, CPAG Ltd

WHAT DO THE FIGURES FROM LOW INCOME FAMILIES STATISTICS SHOW?

The *Low Income Families* statistics show that in the UK in 1992:[12]

- 13,680,000 people – nearly one quarter (24 per cent) of the population of the UK – were living in poverty (on or below income support). Of these, 4,740,000 people – 8 per cent of the population – were living below the poverty line;
- a total of 18,540,000 people – 33 per cent of the population – were living in or on the margins of poverty (up to 140 per cent of income support).

Figure 2.1 shows the rises in the numbers of people living in poverty or on its margins between 1979 and 1992. Due to recent changes in the way the figures are calculated, two sets of figures are given for 1989 (reflecting the old and new methods). Despite these changes, it

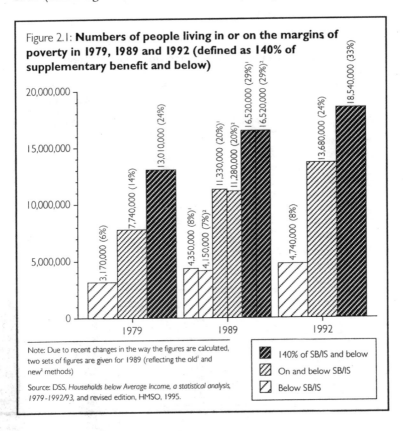

Figure 2.1: **Numbers of people living in or on the margins of poverty in 1979, 1989 and 1992 (defined as 140% of supplementary benefit and below)**

Note: Due to recent changes in the way the figures are calculated, two sets of figures are given for 1989 (reflecting the old' and new' methods)

Source: DSS, *Households below Average Income, a statistical analysis*, 1979-1992/93, and revised edition, HMSO, 1995.

140% of SB/IS and below
On and below SB/IS
Below SB/IS

is nevertheless possible to identify the broad trends since 1979.

In 1979, 14 per cent of the population was living in poverty, but by 1992 this had risen to a quarter (24 per cent). The bulk of this increase occurred in the early part of the decade due to the sharp rise in unemployment. Since 1989, there has been an increase in the numbers in poverty, with increases in both the *numbers* receiving income support and the *numbers* living below income support levels. The *proportion* of the population living below the poverty line has remained relatively constant, while the *proportion* living on income support has increased.[13]

Between 1979 and 1992, the number of pensioners on supplementary benefit/income support fell. However, the number of non-pensioners receiving these benefits – in particular lone parents, couples with children and single persons without children – has increased. Turning to the numbers living below supplementary benefit/income support levels, it is couples with children who account for most of the increase between 1979 and 1992, followed by single people without children and lone parents. The rise in unemployment has accounted for much of the increase in those living on or below supplementary benefit/income support levels since 1979.

LIF includes an analysis which uses a 'constant' or 'fixed' threshold – ie, it scales down the income support threshold to its real 1979 level.[14] Using this approach, there is virtually no rise in the numbers of people living in poverty. However, there is a change in the composition of those living in poverty, with a sharp fall in the number of pensioners and a corresponding increase in non-pensioners.

There are a number of difficulties with this approach. First, the real rise in supplementary benefit/income support is not as large as it appears. When income support took over from supplementary benefit, two of the crucial changes were the replacement of additional payments for needs such as heating and diet with premia for certain groups and the replacement of single payments (grants for one-off needs) with the social fund, which chiefly provides loans. The LIF statistics tend to underestimate the detrimental effect of these changes on some groups as they contain data only on heating additions available in the supplementary benefit scheme, but no others, and do not take into account the change to the social fund at all. Secondly, using a 'constant' or 'fixed' poverty line is to adopt an 'absolute' approach to poverty. As we saw in Chapter 1, this approach is flawed because it assumes that standards of living and our notions of what is essential or necessary do not change and adapt over time.

Such an approach assumes that the poorest should not share in rises in living standards that the rest of society experiences. As the Social Security Committee itself says:

> The long-term rate of supplementary benefit, and the new income support rates together with the range of premiums, provide one guide to society's view on the minimum acceptable living standard for a family who are not in full-time work and who have no other resources. If over time this minimum standard increases, the number of families deemed to be living on minimum income will also rise. To argue otherwise opens up the notion that as the decades go by the minimum acceptable living standard should not rise at all.[15]

HOW MANY CHILDREN?

- In 1992,[16] there were 3,690,000 children – 29 per cent of all children – living in poverty (on or below the income support level). Of these, 830,000 (6 per cent of all children) were living below the poverty line;
- in 1992, there were 4,530,000 children – 35 per cent of all children – living in or on the margins of poverty (below 140 per cent of income support).

A child's risk of falling into poverty depends on the type of family s/he grows up in. In 1992, over three-quarters (78 per cent) of children growing up in lone-parent families were living in poverty compared to 18 per cent of children in two-parent families.

Figure 2.2 shows how the number of children in poverty has grown between 1979 and 1992 and how in 1992 there was a higher proportion of children in poverty in lone-parent families than in two-parent families.[17]

FALLING THROUGH THE SAFETY NET

One of the most important things that the LIF figures reveal is how many people fall through the 'safety net' of income support. In 1992, there were a total of 4,740,000 people (including children) living below the income support level. The largest groups among this total were couples with children and single people without children (the former accounted for 32 per cent of people falling through the safety net and the latter 25 per cent). Many of the single people

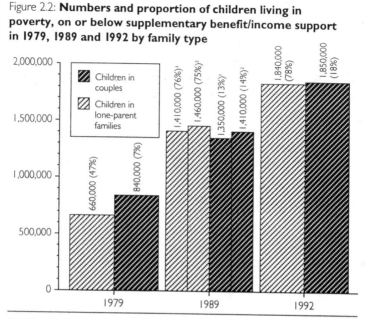

Figure 2.2: **Numbers and proportion of children living in poverty, on or below supplementary benefit/income support in 1979, 1989 and 1992 by family type**

Notes: The percentages show the proportion of children in each family type living in poverty – eg, in 1979, 47% of children in lone-parent families were living in poverty. Two sets of figures are given for 1989 because of methodological changes in the way the figures were calculated. 1989[1] relates to the method used for the 1979 figure also. 1989[2] relates to the method used for the 1992 figure also. Comparisons between 1979 and 1992 should be drawn with caution.

Source: DSS, *Households below Average Income, a statistical analysis,* 1979-1992/93, and revised edition, HMSO, 1995.

living below the income support level were living in households with other adults; they may have been sharing some of their resources and thus might not have been as poor as they appeared to be. Looking at economic status, 27 per cent of people falling below income support level lived in families with a full-time worker; a further 10 per cent of people lived in families with one or more persons working part time.[18] For many of these people, low earnings play a big part in their poverty.

LIF shows just how far people are falling below the poverty line. This is sometimes known as the **poverty gap**. Families below the poverty line are living on average on incomes which are around a quarter lower than income support. However, pensioners tend to have resources of between 80 and 90 per cent of income support while non-pensioners have between 60 and 70 per cent. Couples with children on average live at just under two-thirds of income support.[19]

One of the principal reasons that people are living below the income support level is that they are not taking up means-tested benefits to which they are entitled. Table 2.2 below shows the latest take-up figures for the main means-tested benefits, produced by the Department of Social Security.[20] It reveals that around £2 billion of means-tested benefits went unclaimed in 1992.

TABLE 2.2: **Estimates of take-up of means-tested benefits by case-load and expenditure in 1993/94**

	% take-up by case-load range	% take-up by expenditure range	Total unclaimed (millions) range
Income support	79–88	89–95	£740–£1,660
Housing benefit	88–96	92–97	£230–£690
Family credit	71	81	£230
GB	71–80	74–82	£390–£630

Source: DSS, *Income-related Benefits, estimates of take-up in 1993/94*, HMSO, 1995.

THE SECOND SOURCE: HOUSEHOLDS BELOW AVERAGE INCOME

WHAT ARE THE HOUSEHOLDS BELOW AVERAGE INCOME STATISTICS?

Households below Average Income (HBAI) was published for the first time in 1988. It is now the major source of official information about people living on a low income. The latest edition, *Households below Average Income, a statistical analysis, 1979–1992/93*, was issued in June 1995 and amendments published in October 1995.[21] It examines the living standards of people in the lower half of the income distribution. The series shows:

• the number of individuals in households with incomes below various thresholds, from 40 per cent average household income to average household income;
• the number of individuals living in households in the bottom 10 per cent, 20 per cent, 30 per cent, 40 per cent and 50 per cent of the income distribution (these are known as decile groups), and the rises in real income for each of these groups.

WHAT IS THE POVERTY LINE IN HOUSEHOLDS BELOW AVERAGE INCOME?

Households below Average Income does not contain an obvious poverty line. We have chosen 50 per cent of average income as a poverty line, a definition which is widely used by commentators and in international studies.

HBAI presents figures both before and after housing costs. There are arguments for using both measures.[22] We have chosen in most cases here to use figures which show numbers and income after housing costs for the following reasons. First, the figures are more comparable with supplementary benefit/income support (as these are also after housing costs). Secondly, housing expenditure is different from other kinds of expenditure, varying widely between geographical areas and different stages of life. Thirdly, it is also a fixed cost for many families, particularly those on low incomes, who have little choice about the amount they spend on their housing and therefore about the money they have left, for example, to meet their children's needs.

We show in Table 2.3 a poverty line measured by 50 per cent of average income after housing costs. In 1992/93 (the date of the latest set of figures) a two-parent family with three children aged 3, 8 and 11 were living in poverty if they had an income (after paying for their housing costs) of less than £183 a week. This is equivalent to £196 a week in 1995 prices.

TABLE 2.3: **The poverty line in 1992/93 and expressed in 1995 prices: defined as 50% average income (after housing costs) £ per week**

	1992/93	1995 prices
single person	£61	£65
couple	£110	£118
couple with 3 children (aged 3, 8 and 11)	£183	£196
All family types	£110	£118

Source: Derived from DSS, *Households below Average Income, a statistical analysis, 1979-1992/93*, Government Statistical Service, HMSO, 1995.

WHAT DO THE HOUSEHOLDS BELOW AVERAGE INCOME FIGURES SHOW?

Households below Average Income (HBAI) presents the official figures on low income. HBAI shows that in the UK in 1992/93:

- 14.1 million people were living in poverty (below 50 per cent of average income after housing costs) – one quarter of the population. This is almost three times the number in 1979 – 5 million, or 9 per cent of the population.

WHO IS IN POVERTY?

The global figure of 14 million hides within it important patterns. We can look at the composition of the poor – which groups make up the bulk of those in poverty; we can also assess the risk of poverty – which groups are most likely to be poor. These two things are different – eg, lone parents make up only a small proportion of the total number of people in poverty as they are a small group; however, they have a high risk of poverty.

First we look at the composition of the poor, by economic status and family status. The pie charts on page 35 illustrate how poverty is distributed among different groups (see Figure 2.3).

Looking at economic status first, unemployment is a crucial cause of poverty, accounting for more than a fifth of those in poverty. Couples where both partners are working full time and single people in full-time work make up only 2 per cent of those in poverty. The growing importance of two wages coming in to protect couples and families against poverty is illustrated by the figures which show that couples where only one member is working full time and one not at all make up 9 per cent of those in poverty. People in families where one or more is in part-time work constitute the same proportion of those in poverty – 9 per cent.[23]

Turning to family status, couples with children account for the largest group in poverty – 37 per cent. The next largest group is lone parents who make up 17 per cent of those in poverty.[24] Poverty among lone-parent families has increased dramatically in recent years.

The risk of poverty for different groups is illustrated clearly in Figures 2.4 and 2.5.

The group with the highest risk is the unemployed – three-quarters of them are in poverty. People in families where there is

Figure 2.3: **The composition of the poor (defined as living below 50% of average income after housing costs) in 1992/93**

by family status

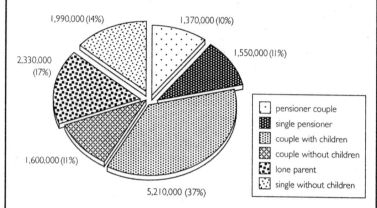

1,990,000 (14%)   1,370,000 (10%)

2,330,000 (17%)   1,550,000 (11%)

1,600,000 (11%)

5,210,000 (37%)

⬚ pensioner couple
▨ single pensioner
⊞ couple with children
▩ couple without children
⠿ lone parent
∴ single without children

by economic status

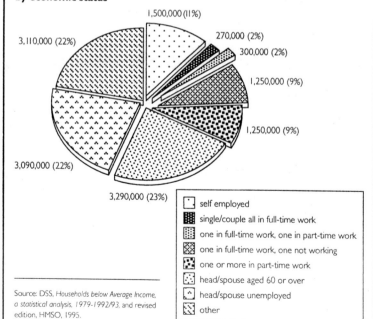

1,500,000 (11%)

3,110,000 (22%)   270,000 (2%)

300,000 (2%)

1,250,000 (9%)

1,250,000 (9%)

3,090,000 (22%)

3,290,000 (23%)

⬚ self employed
▨ single/couple all in full-time work
⊞ one in full-time work, one in part-time work
▩ one in full-time work, one not working
⠿ one or more in part-time work
∴ head/spouse aged 60 or over
⌃ head/spouse unemployed
▨ other

Source: DSS, *Households below Average Income, a statistical analysis, 1979-1992/93*, and revised edition, HMSO, 1995.

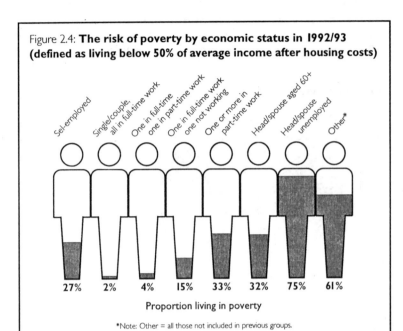

Figure 2.4: **The risk of poverty by economic status in 1992/93 (defined as living below 50% of average income after housing costs)**

27% 2% 4% 15% 33% 32% 75% 61%

Proportion living in poverty

*Note: Other = all those not included in previous groups.

Source: DSS, *Households below Average Income, a statistical analysis, 1979-1992/93*, and revised edition, HMSO, 1995.

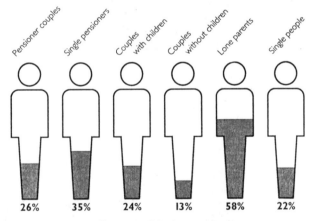

Figure 2.5: **The risk of poverty by family status in 1992/93 (defined as living below 50% of average income after housing costs)**

26% 35% 24% 13% 58% 22%

Proportion living in poverty

Source: DSS, *Households below Average Income, a statistical analysis, 1979-1992/93*, and revised edition, HMSO, 1995.

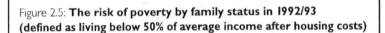

only part-time work also carry a high risk of poverty – one in three.[25] Looking at risk by family status shows that 58 per cent of individuals in lone-parent families are in poverty.[26] The next most vulnerable group is single pensioners where 35 per cent are in poverty. Both the lone parent and the single pensioner group are dominated by women, showing their vulnerability to poverty.

HOW MANY CHILDREN?

Poverty that afflicts children is perhaps the most shocking. The figures below show that children have been more vulnerable to poverty than society as a whole throughout the period from 1979 to 1992/93 (see Figure 2.6).

In 1992/93, a higher proportion of children was living in poverty (defined as below 50 per cent of average income after housing costs) than the population as a whole:[27]

- there were 4.3 million children living in poverty (defined as below 50 per cent of average income after housing costs) – one third (33 per cent) of all children. This compares to 1.4 million in 1979 – 10 per cent of all children.

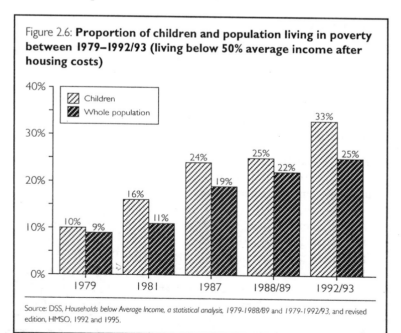

Figure 2.6: **Proportion of children and population living in poverty between 1979–1992/93 (living below 50% average income after housing costs)**

Source: DSS, *Households below Average Income, a statistical analysis*, 1979-1988/89 and 1979-1992/93, and revised edition, HMSO, 1992 and 1995.

WHICH CHILDREN ARE IN POVERTY?

Of the 4.3 million children living in poverty (defined as below 50 per cent of average income after housing costs) in 1992/93:[28]

- 1,250,000 were living in families where there was one or more full-time workers – 29 per cent of all children living in poverty.
- 3,011,000 were living in families where there was no full-time worker – 71 per cent of all children living in poverty. Within this group approximately the same proportion of children were living with couples as in lone-parent families (about 50 per cent of these children lived in two-parent families, and about 50 per cent in lone-parent families).

Children at greatest risk of poverty were those living in families where there was no full-time worker, particularly in large families:

- 76 per cent of children in couples with no full-time worker were living in poverty;
- 71 per cent of children in lone-parent families with no full-time worker were living in poverty.

The risk of poverty was much lower for children in families where there was a full-time worker; however, there was still an increased risk of poverty for large families:

- 6 per cent of children in families with one or more full-time workers and one or two children were in poverty;
- 20 per cent of children in families with one or more full-time workers and with three or more children were in poverty.

WHAT HAS HAPPENED SINCE 1979?

Households below Average Income only provides comparative data as far back as 1979, so we cannot make comparisons over a longer time span. (However, the recent Joseph Rowntree report has looked at changes in incomes over a longer period.[29]) Poverty increased dramatically between 1979 and 1992/93 whether measured before or after housing costs (see Table 2.4).

The HBAI statistics also use a range of 'fixed' thresholds in the same way as the LIF statistics (see p29). The fixed threshold we pick out is 50 per cent of average income after housing costs in 1979, which is increased to allow for inflation. Using this measure, poverty has increased from 5 million to 6.1 million – a rise of 22 per cent.[30]

Some groups show an increased risk of poverty – eg, couples with children and single people without children. Using this constant poverty line, the number of children in poverty has also increased from 1.4 to 1.9 million – a rise of 36 per cent.[31] However, as we outlined earlier, we do not believe that this is the right approach to looking at changes in poverty over time.

TABLE 2.4: **Numbers and proportions of individuals living below 50% of average income before and after housing costs**

| | Before housing costs | | After housing costs | |
	Nos: millions	%	Nos: millions	%
1979	4.4	8	5.0	9
1981	4.7	9	6.2	11
1987	8.7	16	10.5	19
1988/89	10.4	19	12.0	22
1991/92	11.7	21	13.9	25
1992/93	11.4	20	14.1	25

Note: figures for individuals include children

Source: DSS, *Households below Average Income, a statistical analysis 1979–1988/89* and *1979–1992/93* and revised edition, HMSO, 1992 and 1995.

By considering the poorest 10 per cent of the population in 1979 and 1992/93 (after housing costs), we can see how the *composition* of the poorest groups has changed.[32] Figure 2.7 shows how pensioners made up a much smaller proportion of the poorest 10 per cent in 1992/93 than in 1979 (down from 31 per cent to 8 per cent of the bottom 10 per cent); couples with children made up a slightly larger proportion (up from 41 per cent to 47 per cent), as did lone parents (up from 9 per cent to 11 per cent); the proportion of single people without children in the bottom 10 per cent almost doubled between 1979 and 1992/93 (from 10 per cent to 19 per cent). Looking at *economic status*, the effect of unemployment is directly apparent – in 1979 only 16 per cent of the bottom 10 per cent were unemployed, but by 1992/93 the figure had risen to 33 per cent.

GROWING DIVISIONS

The figures also show a stark picture of poor people falling further and further behind the rest of society since 1979 (see Chapter 9 for more detail). Comparing the poorest 10 per cent in 1979 with the poorest 10 per

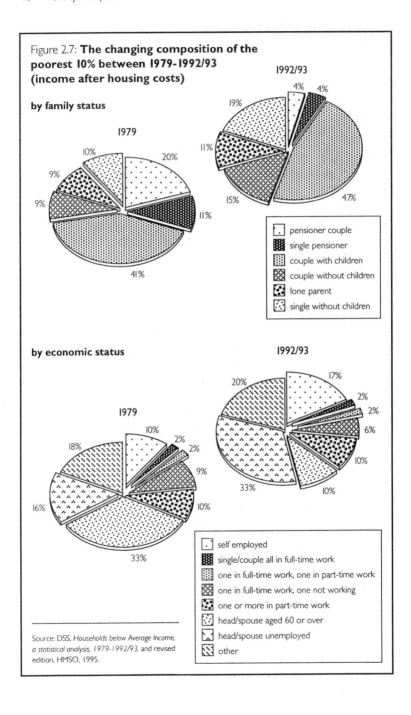

Figure 2.7: **The changing composition of the poorest 10% between 1979-1992/93 (income after housing costs)**

by family status

1979

1992/93

pensioner couple
single pensioner
couple with children
couple without children
lone parent
single without children

by economic status

1979

1992/93

self employed
single/couple all in full-time work
one in full-time work, one in part-time work
one in full-time work, one not working
one or more in part-time work
head/spouse aged 60 or over
head/spouse unemployed
other

Source: DSS, *Households below Average Income, a statistical analysis, 1979-1992/93*, and revised edition, HMSO, 1995.

cent in 1992/93, there was a *fall* in real income after housing costs of 18 per cent, while there was a rise of 37 per cent for the average. These figures include the self-employed. If the self-employed are excluded, the real income of the poorest 10 per cent shows a fall of 10 per cent.[33] Incomes before housing costs also show a very large gap between the poorest and the average – the real incomes of the poorest 10 per cent (including the self-employed) remained the same in comparison with a rise of 36 per cent for the average between 1979 and 1992/93.[34]

HBAI looks at what has happened to the incomes of the poorest 10 per cent. It is important to remember that he people who were in the bottom 10 per cent in 1992/93 are not necessarily the same people who were in the bottom 10 per cent in 1979. However, as Tony Atkinson writes:

> The figures do not mean that any one person has stayed in the [bottom tenth] since 1979 with the same real income. But if the person at this point in 1979 has moved up, then someone else has had a *fall* in real income.[35]

It is the rise in unemployment and self-employment, to a lesser extent, which largely explains the sharp fall in real income after housing costs for the poorest 10 per cent. However, the picture is not a straightforward one: between 1979 and 1992 the *expenditure* of the poorest 10 per cent increased (see Chapter 9 for a fuller discussion).

Poor people's share of total income after housing costs fell between 1979 and 1992/93. The share of the bottom 10 per cent fell from 4 per cent to 1.9 per cent, and the share of the bottom 50 per cent fell from nearly a third (32 per cent) to one quarter (25 per cent). (See Chapter 9 for more detail.)[36]

LIVING ON THE POVERTY LINE

Some suggest that the vast numbers in poverty are due to over-generous poverty lines. The evidence suggests that the level of income measured by both poverty lines is unquestionably meagre in an affluent society. We have looked at what each poverty line represents in cash terms. The poverty line used in HBAI is somewhat higher than that used in the LIF statistics. However, we show that the income represented by both poverty lines cannot provide an adequate standard of living in today's society.

The Family Budget Unit has drawn up a 'modest but adequate' budget standard for different family types, drawing on a panel of experts and consumer groups and using expenditure data.[37]

Items are included in the budget if more than half the population have them or they are regarded as necessities in public opinion surveys. The kinds of items which are included and excluded in this budget standard are listed in Table 2.5. For example, it includes one week's annual holiday in the UK, but excludes a holiday abroad; it includes a sight test but excludes the cost of spectacles.[38] The modest but adequate budget standard can be seen as representing a level of income which allows people to participate fully in society rather than simply exist.

TABLE 2.5: **Modest but adequate budget**

Examples of items included	Examples of items excluded
Basic designs, mass manufactured furniture, textiles and hardware	Antiques, handmade or precious household durables
Prescription charges, dental care, sight test	Spectacles, private health care
Fridge-freezer, washing machine, microwave, food-mixer, sewing machine	Tumble-dryer, shower, electric blankets
Basic clothing, sensible designs	Second-hand, designer and high fashion clothing
TV, video hire, basic music system and camera	Children's TVs, compact discs, camcorders
Second-hand 5-year-old car, second-hand adult bicycle, new children's bikes	A second car, caravan, camping equipment, mountain bikes
Basic jewellery, watch	Precious jewellery
Basic cosmetics, haircuts	Perfume, hair perm
Alcohol – men 14 units, women 10 units (2/3 HEA safety limit)	Smoking
One week annual holiday	Holiday abroad
Walking, swimming, cycling, football, cinema, panto every two years, youth club, scouts/guides	Fishing, water sports, horse-riding, creative or educational adult classes, children's ballet/music lessons

Source: *Social Policy Research Findings*, No. 31, Joseph Rowntree Foundation, November 1992, derived from J Bradshaw et al, *Summary Budget Standards for Six Households*, Family Budget Unit, 1992.

In Table 2.6 we compare the poverty lines represented by income support and 50 per cent of average income after housing costs with the modest but adequate budget standard. It shows that both poverty lines fall below this standard. For example, the income support poverty line for a couple with two children is equivalent to 38 per cent of the modest but adequate budget; 50 per cent of average income represents only 55 per cent.

TABLE 2.6: **A comparison of the modest but adequate (MBA) budget with the income support (IS) and 50% of average income[1] poverty lines (£ per week, 1995 prices)[2]**

	Single man		Couple		Lone mother + 2 children[3]		Couple + 2 children[3]	
Housing (tenants)	35.33	36.46	33.61	34.69	46.34	47.82	46.34	47.82
Council tax	5.29	5.46	7.05	7.28	6.17	6.37	8.23	8.49
Fuel	5.82	6.01	8.36	8.63	14.74	15.21	16.26	16.78
Food	28.09	28.99	41.33	42.65	40.52	41.82	60.92	62.87
Alcohol	8.48	8.75	14.54	15.01	6.06	6.25	14.54	15.01
Tobacco	0.00	0.00	0.00	0.00	0.00	0.00	0.00	0.00
Clothing	6.99	7.21	14.95	15.43	22.91	23.64	29.86	30.82
Personal care	3.93	4.06	9.25	9.55	8.04	8.30	11.45	11.82
Household goods	8.99	9.28	13.86	14.30	22.88	23.61	24.46	25.24
Household services	4.02	4.15	5.79	5.98	4.37	4.51	6.33	6.53
Motoring	36.13	37.29	36.16	37.32	36.67	37.84	39.10	40.35
Fares	3.41	3.52	5.70	5.88	5.43	5.60	11.18	11.54
Leisure goods	6.21	6.41	8.49	8.76	15.20	15.69	15.43	15.92
Leisure services	11.98	12.36	22.96	23.70	13.08	13.50	19.45	20.07
Child care[4]	0.00	0.00	0.00	0.00	69.60	71.83	28.79	29.71
Trade union dues	1.31	1.35	2.60	2.68	1.27	1.31	1.95	2.01
Pets	0.00	0.00	3.65	3.77	6.04	6.23	6.04	6.23
Total for tenants		171.30		235.63		329.53		351.21
Less housing costs[5]		134.84		200.94		281.71		303.39
IS poverty line		46.50		73.00		93.85		115.15
% of MBA budget met		35%		36%		33%		38%
50% average income poverty line		65.00		118.00		113.00		166.00
% of MBA budget met		48%		59%		40%		55%

Notes:
1. After housing costs.
2. The MBA budget has been updated to 1995 prices using the all items retail prices index (this is a slightly different methodology from that used by the Family Budget Unit – see source).
3. Boy aged 10 and girl aged 4.
4. Includes childcare/babysitting costs which are not incurred by everyone.
5. Housing costs are deducted for the purposes of comparison with the poverty lines which are after housing costs.

The MBA budgets are based on model families.

Source: Derived from *Modest But Adequate: summary budgets for sixteen households*, Family Budget Unit, 1995. The Family Budget Unit is now based at King's College, London.

Page 56: Delete from 'The Family Budget Unit…' to 'aged 4 and 10' and insert '(see page 43)'.

In Table 2.6 we compare the poverty lines represented by income support and 50 per cent of average income after housing costs with the modest but adequate budget standard. It shows that both poverty lines fall far below this standard, in particular for families with children. For example, income support for a couple with two children represents only 39 per cent of the modest but adequate budget; 50 per cent of average income represents only 54 per cent.

TABLE 2.6: **A comparison of the modest but adequate (MBA) budget with the income support and 50% of average income[1] poverty lines (£ per week, 1995 prices)[2]**

	Single man	Couple	Lone mother + two young children[3]	Couple + two young children[3]
Housing (tenants)	36.46	34.68	47.82	47.82
Council tax	5.46	7.27	6.37	6.37
Fuel	6.01	8.63	15.21	15.21
Food	28.98	42.65	41.52	41.52
Alcohol	8.75	15.00	6.25	6.25
Tobacco	0.00	0.00	0.00	0.00
Clothing	7.21	15.43	23.64	23.64
Personal care	4.05	9.55	8.29	8.29
Household goods	9.28	14.30	23.61	23.61
Household services	4.15	5.97	4.51	4.51
Motoring	37.29	37.32	37.84	0.00
Fares, etc	3.52	5.88	5.60	12.00
Leisure goods	6.41	8.76	15.69	15.69
Leisure services	12.36	23.69	13.49	13.49
Child care/babysitting[4]	0.00	0.00	71.83	71.83
Trade union dues, etc	1.35	2.68	1.31	1.31
Pets	0.00	3.77	6.23	6.23
Total for tenants	171.28	235.58	329.51	298.07
Less housing costs[5]	134.82	200.90	281.69	250.25
Income support poverty line	46.50	73.00	93.85	115.15
% of MBA budget met by income support	34%	36%	33%	46%
50% average income poverty line	65.00	118.00	113.00	166.00
% of MBA budget met by 50% of average income	48%	59%	40%	66%

Notes:
1. After housing costs.
2. The MBA budget has been updated to 1995 prices using the retail prices index..
3. Aged 4 and 10.
4. Includes childcare costs which are not incurred by everyone.
5. Housing costs are deducted for the purposes of comparison with the poverty lines which are after housing costs.
Source: Derived from *Modest But Adequate: summary budgets for sixteen households*, Family Budget Unit, 1995.

The 13–14 million people who are living in poverty according to either definition are forgoing many of the things that more than half of society takes for granted, whether it is a varied and healthy diet, enough money for transport, new but basic clothing, or treats such as going to the pantomime once every two years. They also fall so far below this level that they are going without many of the most basic essentials.

CONCLUSION

This chapter has looked at bare facts and figures about poverty in the UK. The task of estimating the extent of poverty is made much more difficult because no government of any political colour has established an official poverty line, or attempted to relate rates of benefit to research into people's basic needs.

However, the government has made improvements in how it produces information on low income. In February 1995, the DSS published the first full report of the *Family Resources Survey* (FRS), which provides new material about the household incomes of families with children, unemployed people, elderly people and sick/disabled people. For the first time, a breakdown of some of the data by ethnic origin is also given (see Chapter 6). The DSS is now committed to producing HBAI each year and has provided more extensive material modelling the effects of different assumptions.

Poverty has grown rapidly between 1979 and 1992/93. Whichever poverty line is used, around a quarter of our society was living in poverty in the UK in 1992. The poverty encountered by children is even greater than for society as a whole – around a third of children in the UK were living in poverty in 1992/93. Well over 4 million people were living below the 'safety net' of income support in 1992/93. There have been important changes since 1979, with a decline in the proportion of pensioners in the poorest 10 per cent and a rise in the proportion of single people without children and families with children. While the average person found their income growing very comfortably by 37 per cent between 1979 and 1992/93, the poorest have seen a fall of 18 per cent in their real income (after paying for their housing costs).

The figures we have looked at stop in 1993. Since then there has been a small and slow economic recovery. Nevertheless, unemployment remains high at 2.3 million (August 1995). Earnings inequalities have increased and poverty today is little different from what it was in 1993.

NOTES

1. M Desai, 'Drawing the line', in P Golding (ed), *Excluding the Poor*, CPAG, 1986.
2. DHSS, *Low Income Families 1985*, HMSO, 1988.
3. Social Security Committee, Second Report, *Low Income Statistics: Low Income Families (LIF) 1979-1989*, HMSO, 1993; and Social Security Committee, First Report, *Low Income Statistics: Low Income Families (LIF), 1989-1992*, HMSO, 1995.
4. DSS, *Households below Average Income (HBAI), A Statistical Analysis, 1979-1992/93*, Government Statistical Service, HMSO, June 1995, and revised edition, October 1995.
5. LIF, *see* note 3.
6. Figures for 1989 were revised to take account of methodological changes and corrections to errors, and were published alongside figures for 1991 and 1992. Full details of the revisions are contained in LIF (Appendix 3, *see* note 3). Comparisons with figures for 1979 should be undertaken with caution in light of these changes.
7. LIF, *see* note 3.
8. HBAI, *see* note 4.
9. HBAI, *see* note 4.
10. LIF, *see* note 3.
11. LIF (1979-1989), Appendix 1, *see* note 3.
12. LIF, *see* note 3.
13. LIF, *see* note 3.
14. This is done using the 'Rossi' index, ie, the retail prices index minus housing costs.
15. LIF (1979-1989), para 63, *see* note 3.
16. Derived from LIF, *see* note 3. Note that LIF does not include a breakdown of those on SB/IS by family type for Northern Ireland. This leads to the anomaly that the figures for children *exclude those on SB/IS in N. Ireland*, but include those *below* SB/IS in N. Ireland. They therefore underestimate the extent of child poverty in the UK.
17. *See* notes 15 and 16.
18. LIF, *see* note 3.
19. LIF, *see* note 3.
20. DSS, *Income-related Benefits: estimates of take-up in 1992*, HMSO, 1995.
21. HBAI, *see* note 4.
22. HBAI; refer to Appendix 1 for a fuller discussion of these issues, *see* note 4.
23. HBAI, *see* note 4.

24. HBAI, *see* note 4.
25. HBAI, *see* note 4.
26. HBAI, *see* note 4.
27. HBAI, Table F3 (AHC), *see* note 4.
28. *See* note 27.
29. *Inquiry into Income and Wealth, Volumes 1 and 2*, Joseph Rowntree Foundation, 1995.
30. HBAI, Table E1 (AHC), *see* note 4.
31. HBAI, Table A1, *see* note 4.
32. HBAI, Tables D1 and D2 (AHC), *see* note 4.
33. As HBAI has stated: 'excluding the self-employed may understate the growth in the number of people with low incomes. Overall, it is not possible to be confident whether the results including the self-employed, or those excluding them, give the better indication of the growth in numbers of people with low reported incomes and low living standards.' DSS, *Households below Average Income, a statistical analysis, 1979–1990/91*, HMSO, 1993.
34. HBAI, Table A1, *see* note 4. The changes in real income of the bottom decile are of less certain accuracy due to sampling error and the choice of equivalence scales.
35. A B Atkinson, 'DSS Report on Households below Average Income 1981-1987', paper for the Social Services Select Committee, 1990.
36. HBAI, Table A3, *see* note 4.
37. *Modest but Adequate: summary budgets for sixteen households, October 1994 prices*, Family Budget Unit, 1995.
38. J Bradshaw, L Hicks, H Parker, *Summary Budget Standards for Six Households*, Family Budget Unit, Working Paper No 12, 1992.

3 The causes of poverty

Another local business fails, casual workers are laid off, management is 'thinned out' – unemployment strikes again. A woman works a 50-hour week doing two jobs to scrape together a living. A lone mother struggles on benefit to meet the costs of her child – the only employment on offer would barely pay for her childcare. A man, prematurely retired because of chronic sickness, lives on incapacity benefit which fails to cover his needs. *All these are instances of poverty.*

Poverty is caused by not having access to decently paid employment. It is also the result of the extra costs of having a child or a disability. Poverty is particularly acute when these two factors combine. Moreover, the social security system often fails to meet adequately the needs generated by unemployment, low pay, having a child or coping with a disability. Thus, poverty is also caused by policies – ie, it is avoidable, not just the consequence of random misfortune. The risk of poverty is not shared out evenly – it depends on social class, on gender and on race. We look separately at women (Chapter 5) and race (Chapter 6). Below we explore some of the principal causes of poverty.

UNEMPLOYMENT

There's nothing about now is there? Summat that you just have to live with. I can't see him ever working again now. He'd love to get a job. It'd have to be a miracle. He does anything to work, he's that desperate now.[1]

High levels of unemployment have stubbornly persisted, bringing rapidly growing levels of poverty. In August 1995, the rate of unemployment in the UK stood at 8.1 per cent – 2,292,300 people.[2] This is well over twice as high as the number in April 1979, when there were 1,089,100 unemployed people, a rate of 4.1 per cent.[3]

The method of counting unemployed people is controversial. In the UK, the government uses the 'claimant count' – the number of unemployed people receiving benefits or signing on to get credited national insurance contributions. Any changes in benefit rules are translated immediately into changes in the number of people officially classed as unemployed. According to the Unemployment Unit, the government has changed the method of counting unemployed people 33 times since 1979.[4] Further dramatic changes will be introduced with the jobseeker's allowance in 1996.[5] These changes fall into four broad types: (i) statistical changes such as limiting the count to people actually receiving benefits or contribution credits; (ii) changes in benefit rules; (iii) administrative changes such as tightening up the availability for work test; and (iv) temporary work and training schemes.[6] According to the Unit, the true story of unemployment is much worse than the official version; it estimates unemployment at 11.6 per cent in August 1995 – a total of 3,400,500 people.[7] The government's use of the claimant count has been criticised by the Royal Statistical Society for being an inaccurate measure of unemployment.[8]

The sharp divide between the worlds of unemployed people and those in work does not tell the whole story. Both groups are continually changing in composition, reflecting the growth in both temporary and unstable employment and redundancies in the 1980s. Bill Daniel has described the patterns of recurrent unemployment:[9]

> so far as the unemployed flow as a whole are concerned, they tended to work in low paid, low skilled and manifestly insecure jobs. They lost them with little notice and little or no compensation. Despite the fact that being in work furnished them with relatively poor rewards, they found being out of work was so much worse that they were generally prepared to take the first job offered to them, however unsatisfactory, simply to be back in work. Again, although they tended to be low paid in their previous jobs, they took a pay cut, on average, in order to return to work. Moreover, and perhaps most importantly, for those who found new jobs relatively quickly, those new jobs proved to be only temporary in most cases.

The division of the workforce into 'unemployed' and 'employed' tells only part of the story, however. Since 1986, the numbers of those economically inactive (those, excluding students, who have lost their jobs and withdrawn from the labour market altogether) have exceeded the numbers officially recognised as unemployed.[10] An estimated one third of people who move out of unemployment become economically inactive.[11] Although part of the rise in inactivity can be explained by an increased preference for early retirement, the growth of inactivity among the least skilled and educated members of the labour force suggests that the explanations lie in changes in demand for labour.[12]

Since the early 1980's recession there has also been a polarisation in the distribution of work − between 'work-rich' two-earner households and 'work-poor' no-earner households.[13] Nor is unemployment shared evenly across the country. Particular areas bear the brunt (see Chapter 7 for more detail). For example, in June 1995, unemployment ranged from 11.6 per cent in Northern Ireland to 6.4 per cent in East Anglia.[14]

As well as regional differences, the likelihood of unemployment is also determined by social class, race and sex. For example, in 1993 unemployment rates were three times as high for those previously in manual jobs as for those in non-manual employment.[15] Unemployment rates in the construction industry were substantially higher, at 23.3 per cent, than in the banking sector (6.1 per cent).[16]

In a period of high unemployment, the number of people who are long-term unemployed (for a year or more) increases. Daniel divides the long-term unemployed into three groups: older workers who are near retirement; people who are prone to ill health or not fully fit; and people who are without skills and qualifications.[17] In autumn 1994, 1,106,000 people were long-term unemployed − 44 per cent of all unemployed people.[18] In May 1994, there were 349,000 parents with dependent children who had been unemployed for a year or more. Families sometimes experience multiple unemployment.[19] In 1994/95, some 170,000 families in Britain contained two or more unemployed people.[20] Poverty is most intense among long-term unemployed families because savings are used up, borrowing increases and household goods have to be replaced.

Unemployment means *poverty*. Daniel found that unemployment, however brief, caused both hardship and trauma. When people were asked how they viewed their experience of unemployment, the group as a whole ranked it close to the worst experience they had endured. When asked about the worst things about being out of work, 78 per cent identified lack of money or not being able to afford goods or activities; 60 per cent identified boredom or not having anything to do. Substantial minorities talked of depression and shame.[21] One survey on living standards during unemployment showed that after three months of unemployment the average disposable income of families dropped to 59 per cent of what it had been before unemployment. Families immediately reduced their spending on food, clothing and entertainments. Unemployment was also likely to cause psychological distress: 38 per cent thought that the worst thing about being unemployed was being short of money, but 53 per cent identified being bored, depressed, feeling dependent or losing control as being the prime cause of stress (see Chapter 4).[22] If a man becomes unemployed, there is a strong likelihood that his wife will give up paid work as well. This is because of the benefit rules – if the family is living on income support, a wife's earnings are offset against the benefit pound for pound (after a small amount of earnings is ignored). Thus, the woman would have to be able to command a high wage to make it worthwhile for the whole family to come off benefit. So unemployment in couples often means a sharp drop in income from a two-earner family to no earners at all.[23]

BENEFITS FOR UNEMPLOYED PEOPLE

Unemployed people, rightly or wrongly, accept that they must be content to manage on incomes substantially below those of most people in work. But social justice demands that the gap between earnings and benefits should not be so wide that those without jobs are condemned to an impoverished existence on the margins of society ... The right to decent benefits paid in a dignified manner is no substitute for a job; but as long as jobs are not available for all who seek them, it is an essential requirement.

(Tony Lynes, *The wrong side of the tracks*)[24]

According to the *British Social Attitudes Survey*, the public is less generous in its attitudes to unemployed people than to the elderly. In 1994, 36 per cent of people surveyed wanted government to spend more on unemployment benefits in comparison with 74 per cent for old age pensions. The survey also identifies public misconceptions about levels of benefits: in 1993, only 18 per cent thought that a hypothetical couple on unemployment benefit were 'really poor'; however, when they were told the amount that the couple would receive, the proportion rose to 40 per cent.[25]

In recent years, while unemployment has soared, benefits for unemployed people have been cut. Unemployed people can rely either on *unemployment benefit*, a national insurance contributory benefit, or on *income support* which is means-tested, or on a combination of the two. From October 1996, unemployment benefit and income support for the unemployed will be replaced by a six-month contributory jobseeker's allowance and a means-tested job-seeker's allowance for those unemployed for more than six months. The advantage of contributory unemployment benefit is that it is not means-tested and is paid on an individual basis (so that an unemployed wife can receive unemployment benefit and her husband can continue to work without his earnings affecting her entitlement to benefit). However, because contributions have to be made and unemployment benefit lasts for only a year (six months after April 1996 in line with the introduction of the jobseeker's allowance), many people have been forced on to means-tested income support. In 1993-94, unemployment benefit supported 22 per cent of unemployed people in whole or in part; the rest relied solely on means-tested income support.[26] Some of the cuts and changes made to benefits for unemployed people are:[27]

- In 1980, 5 per cent was cut from unemployment benefit and only restored in 1983.
- In 1980, the earnings-related supplement to unemployment benefit was phased out, and finally abolished in 1982.
- In 1984, the children's additions for unemployment benefit were abolished.
- In recent years, unemployment benefit has dropped as a proportion of average earnings. In 1971 for a single person it was 20.3 per cent of average earnings; this dropped to 18.4 per cent in 1979 and then again to 13.8 per cent in 1994.[28]
- The maximum period of disqualification from unemployment benefit when someone is 'voluntarily unemployed' has increased from six weeks to 26 weeks. During that time income support is *cut* by 20 per cent or 40 per cent of the adult personal allowance.[29]
- On the means-tested side, the 1986 Social Security Act replaced supplementary benefit with income support which is made up of personal allowances with premia for certain groups, such as pensioners, people who are sick or who have a disability, families

with children, and lone-parent families. Unemployed people, however, receive no special premium to supplement their basic benefit.

- The Social Security Acts of 1986 and 1988 also ushered in substantial cuts in benefit for young people. Young unemployed people aged 16 and 17 can only receive income support if they have a Youth Training place or if they fall into one of the strictly defined categories of severe hardship. Otherwise, they have to fend for themselves with little or no support from the state. A lower rate of income support for 18- to 24-year-olds for single and childless claimants was also introduced.

- Since 1988, it has become more difficult to satisfy the contribution conditions for unemployment benefit because benefit rights rely on contributions paid in the two previous years (rather than one) and contributions must be paid rather than credited in at least one of those years. The latter measure particularly affects women who may have been caring for a child or elderly person.

- New rules on availability for work and actively seeking work for unemployed people have deterred many from claiming benefits. The process of claiming and receiving benefits for unemployment has become increasingly stigmatising.[30]

- From April 1996, unemployment benefit will be restricted to six months. From October 1996, the Jobseeker's Act will come into full effect, introducing: the requirement of claimants to agree and sign a jobseeker's agreement (which will identify action that must be taken to find work); tougher 'actively seeking work' and 'availability for work' tests; removal of the automatic payment of income support to those who are disqualified from benefit; and a reduction in contributory benefit for 18- to 24-year-olds.[31]

POVERTY IN EMPLOYMENT

The pay is quite poor but it's better than unemployment benefit, even if it is only for a limited period ... The problem I found with doing casual work is that you have no security, not knowing from one week to the next if your contract will be terminated ... The insecurity of the casual job was the worst problem for me because of all my commitments at home.

(Liz, lone mother of two)[32]

The poverty of low wages and poor working conditions is often still a hidden factor in the poverty debate. Recent government policies have specifically weakened employment rights. In 1982, the Fair Wages Resolution (which set minimum conditions of work for firms operating government contracts) was ended. In 1986, Wages Council protection for young workers was abolished, while, for adult workers, it was weakened. In August 1993, Wages Councils were abolished entirely (with the exception of the Agriculture Wages Board). In addition, the number of wages inspectors was cut substantially in 1986. The legislation to protect low-paid workers has been diluted and the means to enforce what remains of it weakened. The Joseph Rowntree Foundation *Inquiry into Income and Wealth* identifies the growing gap between the high and the low waged. The wages of the lowest paid men remained broadly the same in real terms since 1978 and were lower in real terms in 1992 than in 1975 (see Chapter 9).[33]

Alongside the deregulation of employment law, new patterns of employment have changed the profile of the workforce. There has been a marked increase in self-employment and in part-time and low-paid work and a small increase in temporary work. Women are more likely to be in both part-time and temporary work. Many of these jobs are low-paid with few employment and social security rights – a situation which not only creates poverty, but also stores it up for the future.

Between 1984 and 1994:[34]

- the number of self-employed workers grew by 23 per cent;
- the number of full-time employees grew by 0.1 per cent, while the number of part-time employees grew by 19 per cent. In 1994, 86 per cent of all part-time employees were women;
- the number of permanent workers fell by 8 per cent, while the number of temporary workers grew by 6 per cent. In 1994, women made up 56 per cent of the temporary workforce.[35]

High unemployment and the weakening of employment protection expose workers to low rates of pay. In 1994, over a third (37 per cent) of full-time workers were living on low pay, according to the Council of Europe's decency threshold (£221.50 a week or £5.88 an hour).[36] The risk of low pay is much higher for women and Black and other minority ethnic groups (see Chapters 5 and 6 respectively). Part-time workers are much more likely to be low-paid than full-time workers.

In 1994, using the Council of Europe's decency threshold:

- 4.5 million part-time workers (77 per cent of the part-time workforce) were low paid;
- 5.47 million full-time workers (37 per cent of the full-time workforce) were low paid, and 3.7 million of those were women.

BENEFITS FOR THE LOW-PAID

There are no social security benefits for the low paid as a whole. Housing benefit and council tax benefit are paid to people in low-paid work to help meet their housing costs and their council tax. However, expenditure on housing benefit for people in work has been reduced substantially over recent years.[37] In addition, family credit is paid to families with children in low-paid work. Introduced from April 1988 under the 1986 Social Security Act, it is more generous than its predecessor (family income supplement), but there are still major drawbacks:

- A high proportion of people who are entitled to family credit do not claim. The latest figures show that in 1993/94, 29 per cent of those entitled to claim did not do so.
- Family credit claimants no longer receive free school meals for their children (family income supplement claimants were entitled to free school meals).
- Gains in family credit for many claimants are partially offset by losses in housing benefit and council tax benefit as the family credit is treated as income in the assessment of these benefits.
- Family credit claimants receive no help with mortgage interest payments, unlike income support claimants (whose help with mortgage interest payments has been restricted since October 1995). This pushes some families into the unemployment trap because they are better off on income support than family credit.
- The poverty trap (where a large part of any rise in earnings is withdrawn through increased tax and national insurance and reduced social security benefits) is a particular problem for family credit recipients. The most extreme example is a family which receives family credit, housing benefit and council tax benefit. They will retain only 3 pence of each extra pound that is earned – this is equivalent to a marginal tax rate of 97 per cent.

Although the most extreme form of the poverty trap (whereby someone could lose more than a pound for each extra pound of earnings) has been all but eliminated, the poverty trap now catches more people. In 1985/86, 290,000 families stood to lose between 70 pence and 99 pence out of every extra £1 they earned.[38] By 1993/94, the figure had risen to 640,000.[39]

Disability working allowance is a relatively new benefit which tops up the earnings of people with disabilities in low-paid work; however, it only reaches about 5,200 people. The government is piloting the 'earnings top up' from October 1996 for people without children on low wages. Thus there has been a marked increase in the use of benefits to subsidise wages in recent years.

THE COST OF A CHILD

> I can live on cheese on toast and that doesn't bother me. But the kids have got to eat.[40]

Poverty ebbs and flows through the life cycle, but one particularly vulnerable period is when children are born into the family. Children bring extra costs for essentials and they usually mean that the mother stops work for a while.

The Family Budget Unit at York University has done important work in identifying the direct costs of children. Using a 'modest but adequate' standard of living as the benchmark, Nina Oldfield found that, at October 1994 prices, the weekly cost of a child was estimated to be:

- £61.07 for a child aged 4 or 10 and £62.44 for a child aged 10 or 16 assuming his/her parents are local authority tenants;
- £61.49 for a child aged 4 or 10 and £62.68 for a child aged 10 or 16 living in owner-occupied accommodation.[41]

Parents have experienced rising costs due to the reduction in free services such as transport and leisure. This is particularly so in education where parents are increasingly having to meet the costs of books, stationery, equipment and school trips.[42] The combination of higher costs and lower income pushes families – and particularly lone mothers – into poverty.

Between 1979 and 1992/93, the risk of living in poverty tripled for couples with children, whereas it doubled for couples without children. For lone parents, the risk of poverty is particularly high: 58 per cent of lone parents in 1992/93 were living in poverty, defined as below 50 per cent of average income after housing costs.[43]

BENEFITS FOR FAMILIES WITH CHILDREN

There have been a number of changes of policy in providing benefits for families with children over the last few years. In *Child Benefit: options for the 1990s*, Joan Brown analyses the role of child benefit and its future.[44]

Following the 1987 general election, child benefit – a universal benefit paid to all families – was frozen in real terms for three successive years. However, in 1990 the government announced that child benefit would be increased (though by less than inflation) in April 1991 and its structure changed to include a higher payment for the first/eldest child.[45] In the 1991 Budget, the government announced a further increase for child benefit in October 1991 and a pledge to uprate it in line with prices in future years. Despite these welcome improvements, the cuts in child benefit still have not been made good.

- If child benefit had been uprated in line with inflation from 1979 onwards it would have stood at £10.85 for each child in April 1995. Its value had fallen by 4 per cent (45 pence) in real terms for the eldest child, and 22 per cent (£2.40) for subsequent children.[46]
- The real value of child support (that is, child benefit now, compared with the old family allowances and child tax allowances) for a standard rate tax-paying family is worth less now than 30 years ago (with the exception of a family with one child under 11).[47]
- The government's total saving in 1995/96 from not uprating child benefit in line with prices since 1979, and changing its structure, amounts to £900 million gross and £650 million net.[48]

While child benefit has undergone significant reductions, the government has increased support for children living in families on income support and family credit above the rate of inflation.

However, there is considerable evidence that income support falls far short of providing an acceptable living standard for families with children. The Family Budget Unit drew up a 'modest but adequate' budget (see p42) and found that in 1994 income support provided:

- 32 per cent of a 'modest but adequate' budget (estimated at £358.24 a week) for a couple with two children aged 4 and 10;
- 27 per cent of a 'modest but adequate' budget (estimated at £335.74 a week) for a lone mother with two children aged 4 and 10.[49]

The social fund was introduced in 1987/88 as part of the changes under the 1986 Social Security Act. It replaced the system of entitlements to single payments (one-off grants) with a cash-limited discretionary fund, consisting of interest-free loans and community care grants. Comparing the single payments budget in 1985/86 (before cuts had been introduced) with the community care grants budget in 1995/96 shows a fall of 80 per cent in real terms.[50] The introduction of the social fund has had a detrimental effect on claimants of all types. However, families with children have been hit particularly badly by the social fund because they were more likely to receive single payments under the old system. Many families have found that loans have created considerable hardship, pushing them below the income support level. The Department of Social Security commissioned research into the social fund by the Social Policy Research Unit at York University. Their report is highly critical of the social fund. Among its many findings it showed that people who were repaying loans suffered considerable hardship:

- Almost 70 per cent said that repayments left them with insufficient money to live on.
- Over a third said that they had to cut back on food, clothing or paying bills.
- A fifth borrowed money from other sources to cope with their reduced incomes.[51]

The continuing inadequacies of the social fund have been highlighted in a recent report by the Children's Society, Family Service Units and Family Welfare Association.[52]

DISABILITY AND SICKNESS

To be disabled, therefore, is also to be disadvantaged. It means regularly being unable to participate in the social and economic activities which most people take for granted. It means confronting the negative attitudes of others and sometimes internalising those reactions until they become part of the psychological accoutrements of disability itself. However, at the same time it can also mean gaining the additional insight that comes from encountering a wider range of experiences. It can mean overcoming enormous challenges leading to a sense of achievement and fulfilment.

(*Women and Disability*)[53]

Adults and children with disabilities are frequently locked out of society by a combination of poor employment opportunities, discrimination, lower earnings, high dependency on benefit, greater costs and inadequate services. Together this means that people with disabilities have to live on very low incomes, often with little chance of being able to participate fully in society.

> One of the most significant factors undermining the rights of disabled adults to participate fully and equally in society is their systematic exclusion and marginalisation from the labour market.
>
> (Steven Smith, *Disabled in the Labour Market*)[54]

Research has shown that disabled people are up to three times more likely to be unemployed,[55] reflecting evidence of extensive discrimination in the labour market.[56]

Disabled people in employment are more likely than their non-disabled counterparts to be in low-paid, low-skilled and low-status jobs: 12 per cent are in professional or managerial positions compared to 21 per cent of non-disabled workers, while 31 per cent are in low-skilled manual occupations compared to 21 per cent of non-disabled workers.[57]

The most complete picture of disability in Britain today comes from a survey carried out by the Office of Population Censuses and Surveys (OPCS) between 1985 and 1988.[58] According to the survey, there are 6.2 million adults (14 per cent of all adults) and 360,000 children (3 per cent of all children) with one or more disabilities. The Disability Alliance believes that even this large figure is an underestimate.[59]

Using the OPCS data, it has been estimated that 47 per cent of disabled adults are living in poverty.[60] There are a number of factors contributing to the experience of poverty among disabled people. First, there are the effects on income resulting from labour market exclusion and marginalisation.

The 1993/94 *Family Resources Survey*[61] found that:

- 64 per cent of households with a sick or disabled person received no income from employment;
- 27 per cent of households with a sick or disabled person received all their income from benefits, compared to 10 per cent of households with no sick or disabled person;
- 83 per cent of sick and disabled persons living alone reported

having a gross weekly household income of under £200, compared to 41 per cent of all households.

Disabled people also face additional costs resulting from spending on items and services such as transport, heating, laundry, wear and tear on furniture and clothing, special diets, caring services and prescriptions.[62] The growth of charging for local authority services has a particularly detrimental effect on some disabled people (see p62). The OPCS survey estimated that in 1985:

- 16 per cent of adults with a disability had made a lump-sum purchase for special equipment or furniture related to their disability, averaging £78 over the past year;
- on average, adults with a disability were spending an extra £6.10 a week on regular extra costs such as prescriptions, home services, fuel, clothing and bedding. This extra spending varied with the severity of the disability – £3.20 for people with the least severe disability, rising to £11.10 for people with the most severe disability. On average, 8 per cent of income was spent on disability-related expenses. A number of disability organisations criticised this figure for being unrealistically low.[63]

In addition, disabled people face the risk of poverty because of inadequate benefits.

BENEFITS FOR PEOPLE WITH DISABILITIES

Poor employment chances often mean lifelong dependence on inadequate and patchy social security benefits. Although the government has made some improvements in benefits for people with disabilities, recent years have nevertheless seen a number of cuts:

- Many people with disabilities lost out substantially as a result of the 1988 social security changes. This is because under the supplementary benefit system many people with both mild and severe disabilities received extra weekly payments to help with special diets, extra baths, extra laundry and so on. These additions were replaced by disability and severe disability premiums. Some people with a mild disability – eg, a child with chronic asthma – find they are not entitled to a premium at all. For others, whose extra needs are considerable, the premiums are not sufficient to meet the demands.[64]

- In 1971, invalidity pension for a single person was 20.3 per cent of average earnings; in 1979 it had risen to 23.2 per cent but by 1992 it had fallen to 17.8 per cent.[65] In April 1995, the government introduced a new incapacity benefit, together with the tightening up of administrative and medical control procedures. An estimated 220,000 people are expected to lose benefit as a result of the change.
- There have been considerable problems in achieving successful claims for the disability working allowance, a benefit for disabled people in low-paid work, since it came into operation in April 1992. There are currently only approximately 2,000 claimants. Of these, only a few hundred are claimants who have been encouraged to move into work as a result of the benefit.[66] Take-up of the disability living allowance, a benefit to cover the extra costs of disability, has been better, although there are still some assessment difficulties.[67]

Sickness and disability affect, in turn, how much relatives who take on caring responsibilities can earn; often both carers and people with disabilities are pushed further into poverty. In 1991, almost one in seven adults provided informal care either inside or outside their home.[68] Women were more likely to be carers than men – the British Household Panel study found that, in 1991, 41 per cent of women spent over 50 hours a week caring for someone living with them compared to 28 per cent of men.[69]

OLD AGE

The inequalities experienced in working life – between employment and unemployment, low-paid and high-paid work, and between men and women – are compounded in old age. Broadly speaking, there are still two nations of elderly people. First, there are those who are dependent on income support (the replacement for supplementary pension), living in council or private rented accommodation, with no private or occupational pensions and with few or no savings. At the other end of the spectrum are those who have the generous bonuses of a lifetime's secure and well-paid employment.

In 1993, elderly people (over pension age) numbered 10.6 million in the United Kingdom, or 18 per cent of the population.[70] Because of high unemployment, older people are far less likely to be economically active today than they were 20 years ago and are therefore less able to save or earn in their old age. In 1994/95, retired households were dependent on social security benefits for an average of 51 per cent of their household income (the remainder coming from savings, occupational pensions and small earnings), in contrast to 13 per cent for all households.[71]

Women make up around two-thirds of the elderly population. They are far more likely than men to be poor pensioners because of their lower earnings, interrupted work patterns and greater life expectancy. In 1994, even after adjusting for the different retirement ages, there were over five times as many women pensioners as men dependent on income support.[72]

BENEFITS FOR PENSIONERS

Although elderly people have a very high risk of falling into poverty (see Chapter 2), the government's record on pensions has been mixed. On the one hand, it has increased means-tested benefits for pensioners by over £1.2 billion a year in real terms[73] since 1988. On the other hand, it has introduced fundamental changes which have weakened financial protection for some of the poorest pensioners:

- The decision in 1980 to uprate the retirement pension by rises in prices alone (until that date retirement pension was uprated by earnings or prices, whichever was higher) has meant substantial losses for pensioners. In April 1995, the retirement pension would be £20.30 per week higher for a single person and £33.05 per week higher for a couple had it been uprated by this method since 1980.[74]
- Not surprisingly, the retirement pension has dropped as a proportion of earnings since 1980: the retirement pension for a single person under 80 was 20.3 per cent of adult average earnings in 1971; 23.2 per cent in 1979 and 17.5 per cent in 1994.[75]
- The Social Security Act 1986 both weakened the state earnings related pension scheme (SERPS) and increased incentives to take out a personal pension. The 1995 Pensions Act has weakened SERPS even further, reducing the protection given to people who are least likely to be able to make private provision. In years to come, this will increase poverty for many elderly people. Private pensions mirror inequalities in the labour market, leaving

those who have been unemployed, or low paid, or who have worked part time, in poverty in their old age, while providing large incomes for those who have had permanent and well-paid jobs.

RISING COSTS

A hidden cause of poverty is rising costs; whether it is housing, water rates, the contribution to the council tax, transport, leisure and childcare services, educational materials or school meals. Some of these costs are *partly* covered by income support and housing benefit. Children in families receiving income support are entitled to free school meals. Other costs are not covered by income support – eg, costs at school, leisure and childcare services. The extent to which such benefits do not meet the most frugal estimates of living costs has been highlighted by research.[76]

The situation is particularly acute for those on low incomes, but not on income support, and who face rising costs with no financial assistance. Deregulation, contracting out and privatisation have brought the market into areas that were once heavily subsidised by public money. For example, water prices have risen far above inflation since privatisation. Under strong financial and political pressure local authorities have cut subsidies and increased charges for childcare, leisure services and school meals. Rents have been de-regulated and housing benefit has failed to keep pace with the subsequent increases.

The cost of public transport has risen sharply as government subsidies have been withdrawn. The cost of services, both national and local, is crucial to people's living standards, particularly people living in or close to poverty. Even when charges are presented as voluntary, individuals may feel under pressure to pay. In *Education Divides*,[77] mothers spoke of the pressure they were under to contribute towards voluntary contributions for school trips:

> My daughter had a trip not long ago ... I did write back saying yes she can go on it but how much pocket money does she need? A fiver! I haven't got a fiver spare to give 'er. So she couldn't go on it. My kids don't go on school trips.[78]

Local authorities are increasingly charging for social services such as home helps, day-centre care and meals-on-wheels, although the extent to which certain groups are charged for their care is not consistent across the country.[79] The extra costs of living faced by people with disabilities or chronic illnesses are not always considered when charges are calculated, resulting in considerable financial difficulties for some groups of people.[80]

CONCLUSION

Poverty in the UK is largely determined by three factors – access to the labour market, extra costs, and the failure of policies to deal with them. Access to the labour market depends on a number of factors – among them class, gender and race. We have seen how the rise in unemployment has pushed millions into poverty. Getting a job is not necessarily the way out of poverty if that job pays paltry earnings, entails long hours and has poor working conditions – the poverty of unemployment is simply translated into the poverty of work. Extra costs often come with changes in the life cycle. For example, the extra costs of a child, combined with being out of the labour market, brings poverty to families with children and in particular to lone mothers. Disability and sickness also bring extra costs, but at the same time less or no opportunity to be in paid work. And finally, old age carries a high risk of poverty because it is a time of life when there are few earnings and, as old age progresses, no earnings at all. In each of these cases social security benefits have failed to pull people out of poverty, often leaving them to manage on the most meagre of incomes.

Coming to grips with the causes of poverty involves a commitment to a wide-ranging strategy. CPAG believes that some of the following policies would begin to set the agenda:

- An economic strategy which has the reduction of unemployment at its heart, and which aims to create worthwhile jobs.
- A commitment to training and re-training.
- A statutory minimum wage for full- and part-time workers, equal pay for men and women, pro-rata employment rights for part-time workers.
- A large increase in child benefit and a substantial increase in the availability of affordable childcare.
- A comprehensive disability income which both meets the cost of disability and provides an adequate income for people with disabilities who cannot work or whose ability to work is affected

by their disability.
- Investment in the supply, availability and affordability of housing.
- Replacement of social fund loans by grants based on entitlement.
- Comprehensive civil rights legislation and the enforcement of rights for disabled people which would outlaw discrimination in and out of the workplace.

- Steps towards a non-means-tested social insurance system without restrictive contribution conditions and with individual entitlement to benefits and benefits paid at an adequate level.

NOTES

1. Quoted in E Kempson, A Bryson, K Rowlingson, *Hard times? How poor families make ends meet,* Policy Studies Institute, 1994.
2. Department for Education and Employment, *Employment Gazette, November 1995,* HMSO, 1995.
3. Department of Employment, *Employment Gazette, Historical Supplement No 1, April 1989,* Unemployment Statistics, HMSO, 1989.
4. Personal communication, Unemployment Unit, February 1995.
5. The introduction of the new benefit will reduce the claimant unemployment count by an estimated 25,000 per annum, according to the Unemployment Unit. An additional 45,000 are estimated to lose benefit but remain on the unemployment register while continuing to sign for national insurance contributions credits.
6. T Lynes, *The Wrong Side of the Tracks: Factsheet on unemployment and benefits,* CPAG Ltd, 1992.
7. *Working Brief,* Unemployment Unit, October 1995.
8. *Report of the Working Party on the Measurement of Unemployment in the UK,* Royal Statistical Society, 1995.
9. W W Daniel, *The Unemployed Flow,* Policy Studies Institute, 1990.
10. J Wadsworth, *New Economy Vol 1 Issue 1,* Spring 1994.
11. *See* note 10.
12. *See* note 10.
13. P Gregg and J Wadsworth, *Women, households and access to employment: who gets it and why?,* paper prepared for the Equal Opportunities Commission conference, 10/11 October 1994.
14. Department for Education and Employment, *Employment Gazette, August 1995,* HMSO, 1995.
15. Department of Employment, 'Characteristics of the ILO unemployed', *Employment Gazette, July 1995,* HMSO, 1995.
16. *See* note 15.
17. *See* note 9.
18. Department of Employment, *Employment Gazette, July 1995,* HMSO, 1995.

19. House of Commons, *Hansard*, 15 February 1985, col 701.
20. House of Commons, *Hansard*, 23 November 1995, col 277.
21. *See* note 9.
22. P Heady and M Smyth, *Living standards during unemployment, Vol 1: the results*, HMSO, 1990.
23. For more detail, *see* J C Brown, *Why Don't They Go To Work? Mothers on benefit*, Social Security Advisory Committee, HMSO, 1989, and P Gregg and J Wadsworth, *More work in fewer households?*, Mimeo, NIESR, London, 1994, and *see* note 13.
24. *See* note 6.
25. D Lipsey, 'Do we really want more public spending?' in R Jowell, J Curtice, L Brook and D Ahrendt (eds), *British Social Attitudes: the 12th report*, SCPR, Dartmouth, 1995.
26. *Social Security Department Report: the Government's Expenditure Plans 1995/96 to 1997/98*, Table 7, Cmd 2813, HMSO, 1995.
27. *See* T Lynes (note 6) for full details on cuts to benefits for unemployed people and J C Brown, *Victims or Villains? Social security benefits in unemployment*, Joseph Rowntree Memorial Trust, 1990.
28. *Abstract of statistics for index of: retail prices, average earnings, social security benefits and contributions*, Section 5, DSS, October 1994.
29. D Byrne and J Jacobs, *Disqualified from Benefit*, Low Pay Unit, 1988.
30. *See* note 6.
31. M Barnes and S Witcher, 'The New Seekers', *Poverty 91*, CPAG Ltd, Summer 1995.
32. Quoted in T Potter, *A Temporary Phenomenon*, West Midlands Low Pay Unit, 1989.
33. *Inquiry into Income and Wealth, Volumes 1 and 2*, Joseph Rowntree Foundation, 1995.
34. *See* note 14.
35. Derived from Department of Employment, *Employment Gazette, June 1995*, HMSO, 1995.
36. The Low Pay Unit, *The New Review*, No 30, November/December 1994.
37. Support with housing costs has been reduced as a result of reductions in mortgage interest payments for claimants on income support and changes to housing benefit calculations.
38. House of Commons, *Hansard*, 10 December 1992.
39. Social Security Departmental Report, *The Government's Expenditure Plans 1995/96 to 1997/98*, CM 2813, HMSO, 1995.
40. Mother of two children under five, quoted in S Middleton, K Ashworth and R Walker, *Family Fortunes: pressures on parents and children in the 1990s*, CPAG Ltd, 1994.
41. N Oldfield, personal communication, August 1995.
42. T South and M Noble, *Education Divides: poverty and schooling in the 1990s*, CPAG Ltd, 1995.

43. DSS, *Households below Average Income Statistics 1992/93*, HMSO, 1995.
44. J C Brown, *Child Benefit: options for the 1990s*, Save Child Benefit, 1990.
45. *Child Benefit: looking to the future*, Coalition for Child Benefit, 1991.
46. House of Commons, *Hansard*, 20 November 1995, col 32.
47. House of Commons, *Hansard*, 20 November 1995, col 31.
48. House of Commons, *Hansard*, 20 November 1995, col 32.
49. *'Modest but Adequate': summary budgets for sixteen households, October 1994 prices*, Family Budget Unit, 1995. *See* previous edition of *Poverty: the facts* for low-cost budget.
50. House of Commons, *Hansard*, 8 November 1995, col 1023.
51. M Huby and G Dix, *Evaluating the Social Fund*, and R Walker, G Dix and M Huby, *Working the Social Fund*, HMSO, 1992.
52. *Out-of-pocket – the failure of the social fund*, Children's Society, Family Service Units and Family Welfare Association, 1996.
53. S Lonsdale, *Women and Disability*, Macmillan, 1990.
54. S Smith, *Disabled in the Labour Market*, Economic Report, Vol 7, No 1, Employment Policy Institute, July/August 1992.
55. *See* R Berthoud, J Lakey and S McKay, *The Economic Problems of Disabled People*, Policy Studies Institute, 1993.
56. *See* note 54.
57. *Disability and Discrimination in Employment*, RADAR, 1993.
58. OPCS, *Surveys of Disability in Great Britain, Reports 1-6*, HMSO, 1988/89.
59. Disability Alliance, *Briefing on the 'First Report' from the OPCS Surveys of Disability*, 1988.
60. *See* note 55.
61. DSS, *Family Resources Survey*, Government Statistical Service, 1995.
62. *See*, for example, L Grant, *Disability and Debt: the experience of disabled people in debt*, Sheffield Citizens Advice Bureaux, 1995.
63. *See* note 58.
64. *See* R Cohen, J Coxall, G Craig and A Sadiq-Sangster, *Hardship Britain: being poor in the 1990s*, CPAG Ltd in association with FSU, 1992, for case studies.
65. *See* note 28.
66. K Rowlingson and R Berthoud, *Evaluating the Disability Working Allowance: first findings*, Policy Studies Institute, 1994.
67. R Sainsbury, M Hirst, D Lawton, *Evaluation of Disability Living Allowance and Attendance Allowance*, DSS Research Series Report No 41, HMSO, 1995.
68. L Corti and S Dex, 'Informal carers and employment', Department of Employment, *Employment Gazette, August 1993*, HMSO, 1993.
69. *See* note 55.
70. OPCS, *Population Trends 80*, HMSO, Summer 1995.

71. *Family Spending, A report on the Family Expenditure Survey, 1994-95*, HMSO, 1995.
72. DSS, *Social Security Statistics 1995*, HMSO, 1995.
73. House of Commons, *Hansard*, 6 November 1995, col 646.
74. House of Commons, *Hansard*, 6 November 1995, col 648.
75. *See* note 28.
76. *See*, for example, N Oldfield and Autumn C S Yu, *The Cost of a Child: Living standards for the 1990s*, CPAG Ltd, 1993.
77. *See* note 42.
78. *See* note 42.
79. *Charging Customers for Social Services: local authority policy and practice*, National Consumer Council, 1995.
80. *See* note 79.

4 Dimensions of poverty

Poverty curtails freedom of choice. The freedom to eat as you wish, to go where and when you like, to seek the leisure pursuits or political activities which others expect; all are denied to those without the resources ... poverty is most comprehensively understood as a condition of partial citizenship.

(Peter Golding, *Excluding the Poor*)[1]

Poverty filters into every aspect of life. It is not simply about doing without things; it is also about being denied the expectation of decent health, education, shelter, a social life and a sense of self-esteem which the rest of society takes for granted.

In this chapter we look at some dimensions of poverty: living on a low income, debt, poor health and homelessness.

LIVING ON A LOW INCOME

Living on benefit or on low earnings creates material and social hardship. We look at just what it means to have to survive on a very tight budget for extended periods: going short of the essentials, being isolated, unable to meet children's needs, living with stress and dealing with the benefit authorities. But by highlighting the impact of poverty, the tendency is to ignore the countless strategies that claimants and others have for coping. These may be informal networks between women to share childcare, run toddlers' groups and set up small-scale cooperatives; or initiatives to recycle secondhand goods; or establishing credit unions and community enterprises; or running youth clubs and old people's lunch clubs.[2]

A number of qualitative studies graphically highlight both the experience of poverty and the strategies people evolve for coping with living on low incomes.[3]

GOING SHORT

Many studies have shown how people on low incomes have to cut down on essentials such as food, clothing, fuel and household goods. A study of living standards of 60 families with children by Lydia Morris and Jane Ritchie found that families on lower incomes found it difficult to balance budgets, frequently ran out of money before the next giro arrived, often borrowed from others or fell into arrears:

> At the lowest resource levels there are couples who regularly go without food, have difficulty clothing children, have to deny them recreational spending, and are severely constrained and sometimes thrown into further debt by conventional celebrations.[4]

Hard Times by Elaine Kempson *et al* analyses the budgeting strategies of 74 families with children living on low incomes.[5] They identified the ways 'families were forced to assign priorities within their necessities' such as food:

> I don't cut down, as I say, with the kids. I try to make sure they get, but like I cook a meal and as long as there's plenty for them, I make do with a piece of toast. (Sally, quoted in Kempson *et al*, *Hard Times*)[6]

or clothing:

> We haven't had clothing since I've been out of work, have we? ... Winter will be a problem because none of use have got a coat or jumpers or anything. (Glen, quoted in Kempson *et al*, *Hard Times*)[7]

or fuel:

> I try to cut down on me electric. Many a Sunday afternoon our electric has gone. We've just waited 'til Monday. (Trudy, quoted in Kempson *et al*, *Hard Times*)[8]

In 1991, the National Children's Home's *Poverty and Nutrition Survey*, a study of 354 families with children on low incomes, found that one in five parents and one in ten children had gone without food in the previous month because they did not have enough money to buy food.[9]

ISOLATION

Hardship Britain describes the sense of isolation and exclusion that many people in poverty experience:

> Like the children, adults often found their social life severely limited. In general, people had very little money to socialise with friends and were therefore often deprived of much social contact outside the home. The exceptions were people who clearly had a strong network of local friends and/or family.[10]

Only a minority of families interviewed in *Hardship Britain* had any money left over for social activities; most could not afford to go out or invite people:

> It's very shameful when you can't treat your guests good and feed them well ... The government only gives a little bit of money which isn't even enough to feed yourself, let alone anyone else that comes to the house.[11]

This is confirmed by *Hard Times*, which found that many families in poverty saw social activities as a luxury and reduced their spending accordingly:

> I haven't had a holiday for about seven years, apart from one week in a caravan ... I couldn't afford to save to go on holiday, I'd have to start saving two years beforehand. (Kelly, quoted in Kempson *et al*, *Hard Times*)[12]

The *Family Expenditure Survey* confirms these experiences.[13] Families on low incomes spend less on the so-called 'extras'. In 1994/95:

- lone parents in the bottom fifth spent £4.78 a week on leisure services (5.1 per cent of their weekly expenditure after housing), couples with children in the bottom fifth spent £13.61 (7.5 per cent) compared to £31.20 (13.2 per cent) for all households;
- lone parents in the bottom fifth spent £4.84 on average a week on motoring (5.2 per cent of weekly expenditure after housing), couples with children in the bottom fifth spent £23.96 (13.2 per cent) compared to all households £36.17 (15.3 per cent).

THE IMPACT ON CHILDREN

> Childhood remains a time of great vulnerability as well as great promise.
> (E Alberman, in *The Health of our Children, Decennial Supplement*)[14]

Poverty has both an immediate effect and a long-term impact on the course of children's lives. Despite the attempts of parents, in particular mothers, to shield their children from the worst effects of poverty, children inevitably suffer from the hardships that accompany living on very little money. *Hardship Britain* documents the way in which families could not afford to send their children on school trips or outings with friends:

> We can't afford to send the children on school trips, so they stay at home for the day.

> There's no extras, I can't afford to go with friends' families to McDonald's for tea. (Quoted in Cohen *et al*, *Hardship Britain*)[15]

Many said that there were few play facilities for children and they had no money to travel further afield.

Family Fortunes by Sue Middleton *et al* found that children from less affluent homes were much more likely to go on holiday in the UK rather than abroad; to have shorter holidays; and to be more dependent on day trips from school for their experience outside home than children from more affluent homes.[16] The research also revealed that children from less affluent homes watched more television (around three hours more per day) than their more affluent counterparts. This may be related to having less money for a broader range of activities.

Aside from the immediate experience of poverty, there is a great deal of evidence to show that poverty and deprivation have a long-term impact on children's life-chances. In *The Health of our Children, Decennial Supplement*, there is a wealth of material about trends in children's health. While in many respects children's physical health has improved, the report states:

> there is abundant evidence that the quality of children's health is threatened by a multitude of new problems of many different types, the pervasive effects of adverse demographic, economic, cultural developments and changes in priorities.[17]

This is confirmed by a Barnardo's report, *All Our Futures* by Sally Holtermann, a major study of the impact of government policies on children and young people.[18] She concludes that:

> Children from poor homes have lower life expectancy and are more likely to die in infancy or childhood; they have a greater likelihood of poor health, a lower chance of high educational attainment, a

greater risk of unemployment, a higher probability of involvement in crime and of enduring homelessness. Girls from poor homes are at greater risk of teenage pregnancy.[19]

Poverty moulds children's futures; however, the role of parents is also crucial. A number of authors have argued that poverty affects children partly by diminishing parents' capacity and resources to bring up their children:

> Good parenting requires certain permitting circumstances. There must be the necessary life opportunities and facilities. Where these are lacking even the best parents may find it difficult to exercise their skills. (Rutter, quoted in Utting, *Family and Parenthood: Supporting families, preventing breakdown*)[20]

STRESS

Many people who have had to live on low incomes for long periods talk of suffering from anxiety, strain and stress. Coping on very little money often created difficulties for relationships within couples and between parents and children.

> You end up pulling your hair out because you can't ever get away for a night out like working people ... Tensions build when you get a bit of time on your own.

> The children are always asking for things – they say their friends have this and this ... we have to say no, so the children get upset and we feel upset.
>
> (both quoted in *Hardship Britain*)[21]

Above all, some claimants talked of the way that lack of money brought a loss of control and diminished self-confidence:

> I think that the real problem of being on the dole is it destroys your self-esteem, you know, and your ability to provide for yourself ... I said lack of self-esteem but I mean also, like, a lot of apathy. If you're on the dole for a long period of time you tend to get ... quite apathetic in many ways.[22]

BATTLING WITH THE BENEFIT AUTHORITIES

Living on a low income, coming on and off social security, involves vast quantities of form-filling, visiting benefit offices, queueing and sorting out difficulties.[23] Benefit authorities, while they are there to help, all too often are a burden in themselves because of the demands they place on claimants. *Hardship Britain* documents the ways in which many claimants feel stigmatised because of their experience of the social security system and how some give up in the face of past failures to gain entitlement:

> Claimants emphasised that they found direct dealings with the DSS difficult and stressful, especially if they had to call at the office – often having to wait hours to be seen – rather than telephone. The atmosphere of the waiting rooms ... discouraged many of them from going there.[24]

Local Benefits Agency offices have replaced local DSS offices. While its commitment to providing a better service is a positive development, many of the difficulties are likely to remain: shortage of resources, rising unemployment and extensive and complex means-testing.

Living on a low income means cutting down on basics, it means no money for treats for the children, it means having to rely on friends and relatives to come to the rescue; it sometimes means being isolated and coping with a battered sense of self-esteem.

DEBT

> Debt results from either a sudden disruption to income (for example, as a result of unemployment or relationship breakdown or illness), where previous commitments are difficult to sustain, or from a slower, cumulative effect of a persistently low and inadequate income (for example, as a result of living on benefit for a sustained period), and it is these two processes that have been so pronounced during the 1980s. The processes of slow decline and sudden disruption are conceptually distinct, although in practice linked for many households.
>
> (Janet Ford, *Consuming Credit: debt and poverty in the UK*)[25]

INDICATORS OF DEBT

Debt is a major problem in the UK:

> One of the things that could go wrong is our daughter could lose her job. Without her contribution we couldn't pay enough. She doesn't have to help us, she isn't living here. But if we keep it up, and

everything stays as it is now we will clear the arrears over 19 and a half years. That's what the judge agreed. The regime has to be kept up. If we miss they'll take it from us, which is what they want to do. I told you that at the start. But we live at rock bottom. We couldn't squeeze another penny. Even now we break the rules to get more money and there have been odd weeks when we've missed [the mortgage] but we've always made it up quickly, usually the next week.

(Mr and Mrs X, two teenage children and one older child living away from home quoted in J Ford, *Which Way Out?*
Borrowers with long-term mortgage arrears)[26]

- In 1994, 49,210 homes were repossessed – up from 12,400 in 1984. In 1994, 133,700 homeowners were between six and 12 months in arrears with their mortgage payments compared with 42,810 in 1984.[27]

- Government policies, which have steadily restricted support for homeowners on income support, are likely to increase both the levels of arrears and repossessions.

- In 1992, one in five homeowners who had bought their properties in the last five years owed more than their property was worth.[28]

- In 1994/95, 10,047 domestic customers in England and Wales had their water supplies disconnected for non-payment of charges. Although this represents a fall in recent years, in 1989/90, the comparable figure was 8,426.[29]

- In 1994/95, there were 848 electricity disconnections in England and Wales, down from 98,894 in 1979/80. In 1994, there were 16,308 gas disconnections, a 4 per cent increase since 1992 but a fall from 35,166 in 1979.[30] The decrease in disconnections for fuel has been accompanied by a substantial increase in pre-payment meters. Such meters allow customers effectively to disconnect themselves if they are short of money. Thus the official figures hide the true extent of fuel poverty.[31]

A CAB in Yorkshire reported a 49-year-old woman in poor health who is virtually housebound because of arthritis and a hip injury. She also has angina and a recurring kidney problem which requires regular in-patient treatment. She had direct payments of £11.15 for gas, £6.90 for electricity, £3.24 for water, £2.15 for community charge and £4.25 for social fund repayments. This left her with £14.76 a week to live on.

(quoted in NACAB, *Make or Break?*, *CAB evidence on deductions from benefit*)[32]

Many income support claimants are living below the basic benefit level because of direct deductions for arrears. Deductions can be made for an increasing number of arrears: rent, water charges, fuel charges and the council tax, mortgage and other housing costs, accommodation charges. On top of arrears, deductions can be made for current consumption (eg, for fuel and water), for repayment of social fund loans and for punitive sanctions such as fines for not co-operating with the Child Support Agency. While there is a ceiling on the total amount which can be deducted for certain arrears (£7.05 per week from April 1995), the ceiling does not include the amount for current consumption. Up to 25 per cent of benefit can be deducted from the claimant for fuel, rent, water and mortgage interest arrears without permission. Although there are no official statistics which show how many claimants are facing multiple deductions, there are indicators of how many income support claimants have deductions for certain items.[33] In 1994:

- 44,000 income support claimants had electricity deductions at an average weekly amount of £11.99; 185,000 had gas deductions at an average rate of £10.49 per week;
- 151,000 income support claimants had automatic deductions to pay their rent arrears and other housing costs at an average of £4.90 per week;
- 663,000 income support claimants had automatic deductions to repay social fund loans at an average of £6.37 a week;
- 33,000 income support claimants had direct deductions from their basic benefit to pay council tax arrears at an average of £2.30 per week;
- 217,000 income support claimants had direct deductions for water and sewerage charges at an average of £5.83 a week;
- 34,000 income support claimants had direct deductions for child support at an average of £2.33 per week.

The proliferation of deductions which can be made from income support has led to an intolerable situation where claimants are left with income insufficient to support even a subsistence level of existence.

(NACAB, *Make or Break?, CAB evidence on deductions from benefit*)[34]

The National Association of Citizens Advice Bureaux attributes the rise in deductions to increasing unemployment, higher bills, and new deductions. While many claimants like deductions because they help with budgeting, NACAB argues that they are problematic because benefits are too low.[35] A survey conducted for the DSS found that deductions increased with length of time on benefit: a third of the sample had more than one deduction; and that only 40 per cent of those with deductions reported that they had enough to live on, 26 per cent had not quite enough and 32 per cent definitely did not have enough to live on.[36]

WHO FALLS INTO DEBT?

Not surprisingly, many of the poorest households face acute debt problems. In *Credit and Debt in Britain, the PSI Report*, Richard Berthoud and Elaine Kempson defined debts as difficulties in paying household expenses or consumer credit payments.[37] If a family said they had a problem meeting an expense, this counted as a problem debt, and three or more of these counted as multiple debt. The authors show how a third of households with net weekly incomes of less than £100 had debts, compared with 2 per cent for households with incomes of above £400 a week (see Table 4.1):

TABLE 4.1: **Incidence of problem debts by income for non-pensioner households (%)**

Net weekly income	Proportion with problem debts	Proportion with multiple debts
up to £100	33	10
£100-150	22	4
£150-200	13	4
£200-250	9	2
£250-300	10	1
£300-400	8	1
£400 or more	12	–

Source: R Berthoud and E Kempson, *Credit and Debt in Britain, the PSI Report*, Policy Studies Institute, 1992.

However, some families are more likely to be in debt than others. Berthoud and Kempson identify three 'debt–inducing' factors: age, children and income. Any two of these factors brought a much higher risk of debt – eg, young households with low incomes or families with children on low incomes. Lone parents are particularly at risk: they had three times the number of problem debts as single people without children. The majority of debts faced by people living on low incomes are not the result of excessive consumerism –

rather, as Berthoud and Kempson put it:

> Low income leads to indebtedness through the week-to-week budgeting problems it causes, rather than because poor people persist in buying consumer goods they cannot afford.[38]

THE IMPACT OF DEBT

> If I know that we ain't got no food, and the gas man's waiting, I'm sorry, I'm going to buy my shopping. They're OK. The gas will survive. We won't ... no matter what, my family always comes before a bill. I just phone up and say I'm going on holiday for a fortnight and I'll sort it out when I come back. You know, I think of some lies to tell them.
>
> (Laura, quoted in Kempson *et al, Hard Times*)[39]

Hard Times found that families on low incomes adopted two ways of managing: either they reduced their spending on essentials or they got into debt – 'bill juggling', which was particularly detrimental in terms of stress and anxiety.[40] This is borne out by Lydia Morris and Jane Ritchie's study, which shows that getting into debt was the only way of coping for some of the poorest families.[41] Income support claimants had loans for essential household goods such as beds, bedding, washing machines, cookers, fridges and carpets:

> While the use of debt or credit is almost universal, in extreme cases, people are only able to clothe their children, or replace a broken cooker through loans or credit, by entering into debt. The short term effect on the achieved standard of living has to be offset against the long-term strain (both financial and psychological) of servicing what can otherwise be spiralling commitments.[42]

Debts often lead to yet further debt. The pressure of having to meet urgent demands often drives people into seeking 'secured' loans on their homes or borrowing from money lenders. The first brings with it the danger of losing your home, the second exorbitant rates of interest. A survey in Birmingham of licensed money-lenders to the unemployed and people on benefit found that they had an average of 525 per cent annual percentage rate interest.[43]

> We were doing well until a year ago, then we had loans to pay off, loans for necessities. You're sinking the whole while.
>
> (Quoted in L Morris and J Ritchie, *Income Maintenance and Living Standards*)[44]

Debt is still frequently regarded by society at large as a sign of personal failure and it is this which adds to the stress, anxiety and stigma which accompany debt. *Deep in Debt*, the NCH survey of 347 families, looked at the effects of worries about money: 71 per cent of respondents were depressed; 50 per cent were unable to sleep; 40 per cent felt that they could not cope; 39 per cent smoked more; 21 per cent felt that their relationship with their partner had been damaged. Many people felt embarrassed and guilty about being in debt.[45] Janet Ford sums up the impact of debt:

> The experience of debt magnifies and reinforces the experience of poverty – the watchfulness and anxiety over money; the calculation and moving around of limited funds. But debt may also alter the agenda. For example, social exclusion may increase; households become vulnerable to legal sanctions and to the loss of any property they possess; homelessness cannot be discounted.
>
> (Janet Ford, *Consuming Credit: debt and poverty in the UK*)[46]

POOR HEALTH

The international evidence on inequalities in health is compelling. People who live in disadvantaged circumstances have more illnesses, greater distress, more disability and shorter lives than those who are more affluent. Such injustice could be prevented, but this requires political will. The question is: can British policy makers rise to the challenge?
(M Benzeval *et al* (eds), *Tackling Inequalities in Health: an agenda for action*)[47]

INDICATORS OF INEQUALITIES IN HEALTH

MORTALITY STATISTICS

While there has been a significant decline in infant mortality as a whole, the gap between rich and poor remains substantial. *Mortality Statistics; Perinatal and Infant: social and biological factors* is published annually by the Office of Population Censuses and Surveys.[48] Table 4.2 shows the rates of perinatal and infant mortality by social class for births within marriage.

Perinatal mortality figures show that in 1992, nine out of every 1,000 babies born into Social Class V (unskilled workers) were still-born or died in the first week of life; this compares to six out of every 1,000 babies born into Social Class I (professional occupations). The figures for infant mortality (deaths occurring in the first year of life) show similar disparities – eight out of 1,000 babies born into Social Class V died in their first year, compared to five out of 1,000 for Social Class I. The gap between social classes for both perinatal and infant deaths has remained broadly static between 1979 and 1992. However, the differential between social classes is likely to be underestimated because it includes legitimate births only.

TABLE 4.2: **Perinatal and infant mortality rates per 1,000 total births 1978-79 and 1992 compared by social class (for births within marriage only)**

	Perinatal		Infant	
Social Class	1978-79	1992	1978-79	1992
I	11.9	6.3	9.8	5.0
II	12.3	6.1	10.1	4.6
III non-manual	13.9	6.8	11.1	5.5
III manual	15.1	7.0	12.4	5.6
IV	16.7	7.4	13.6	5.8
V	20.3	8.9	17.2	7.9
Other	20.4	10.2	23.3	10.5
Ratio of social class V: I	1.71	1.7	1.8	1.6

Source: *Mortality Statistics, Perinatal and Infant: social and biological factors, 1978-79 and 1992*, Office of Population Censuses and Surveys, HMSO, 1995

Inequalities between rich and poor extend throughout the lifespan. According to a recent government report, *The Health of the Nation, variations in health: what can the Department of Health and the NHS do?*:

- life expectancy at birth is around seven years higher in Social Class I than social class V;
- children in Social Class V are four times more likely to suffer accidental death than those in Social Class I;
- 62 of the 66 major causes of death among men were more common in Social Classes IV and V than in other social classes;
- 64 of the 70 major causes of death among women were more common in Social Classes IV and V than in other social classes;
- a number of studies have shown increasing socio–economic differentials in mortality rates over recent years.[49]

Not only are there differences in mortality rates between social classes, but also between men and women, different minority ethnic groups and regions.

UNEMPLOYMENT AND HEALTH

Unemployment begets poverty, which begets ill health and premature death. Any lingering doubts about this genealogy were settled in England and Wales by a longitudinal study of mortality and social organisation, which explains much of the excess mortality experienced by men seeking work.

(R Smith, 'Poor Britain: Losing Out', *British Medical Journal*)[50]

The evidence that unemployment kills – particularly the middle-aged – now verges on the irrefutable.

(R Smith, 'Unemployment: here we go again', *British Medical Journal*)[51]

There is growing evidence of the health risks of unemployment. According to the *British Medical Journal*, death rates are particularly high from suicide, accidents, violence and circulatory diseases. International studies have confirmed this picture: a study in Finland in 1990 showed that mortality was 90 per cent higher among the unemployed than the employed (after other factors were controlled for) and that mortality increased with longer durations of unemployment. A study in Sweden showed raised cholesterol and blood pressure in unemployed men. There is also mounting data on the psychological effects of unemployment: redundancy brings on depression and anxiety; economic difficulty increases the risk of such depression.[52] Research has shown that one in five unemployed people report that their mental health has deteriorated and that as unemployment continues the risk of psychiatric illness increases.[53]

Unemployment tears at the routine foundation of a person's use of time and creates a demand for multiple changes in his or her lifestyle and perspective of the world. The individual's reaction to long-term unemployment may manifest itself in ... depression, alcohol abuse and even suicide.' (*Nursing Times*, 27 July 1994)

Interestingly, new research suggests that it is crucial to look not just at unemployment, but also at the quality of work which is performed. It appears that low control, little variety and use of skills at work are all related to poorer health outcomes.[54]

ILLNESS

> There are ... more general health problems noted by couples on income support ... These mostly concern depression and stress related to financial difficulties, though children's health in some cases suffers because of poor housing.
>
> (L Morris and J Ritchie, *Income Maintenance and Living Standards*)[55]

Poverty not only brings the risk of a shorter life-span, but it also means that the lives of adults and children are more likely to be ground down by illness and disability.

There are well-established links between illness ('morbidity statistics') and social class. The *General Household Survey* examines these patterns, which it breaks down by sex and occupational grouping.[56] The Survey found that self-reported long-standing illness ranged from 28 per cent of professional men and 25 per cent of professional women to 40 per cent of unskilled male manual workers and 42 per cent of unskilled female manual workers. Other research reinforces this finding. A British heart study found that angina was twice as high among male manual workers than male non-manual workers in their middle age. The same study found that lung function was also worse in manual groups (this was partly independent of smoking patterns). Other studies have found that self-reported disability is twice as high in Social Class V as Social Class I.[57]

Hardship Britain documented the frequent occurrence of health problems among people living on income support: over 65 per cent of the families interviewed by the Family Service Units reported ill-health or disability among parents, and over 70 per cent among children. Almost two-thirds of families interviewed in the Bradford study (also described in *Hardship Britain*) reported long-term sickness or disability. Asthma, bronchitis and eczema were the most commonly reported conditions in both studies. The studies found that ill-health was associated with the stress caused by poverty, with the inability. to meet extra expenses caused by certain illnesses and not being able to heat homes sufficiently to be able to relieve certain conditions.[58]

> When you're down your health goes down. When you know you're worried that's the next stress, because stress causes illness. You'll find a lot of people are sick who's poor because they've got a lot of stresses and if you lift them up a few bob it helps, it really does help.
>
> (Lone parent quoted in *Hardship Britain*)[59]

In *All our Futures*, Sally Holtermann documents key trends in children's overall health; while there have been important improvements in health, such as the decline in death rates (seen above) and infectious diseases, there remain substantial inequalities between children in different social classes:

- there is a slight increase in the number of parents reporting long-standing illness that limits activity among their children between 1979 and 1991 and a growth in the incidence of asthma;
- children in manual social class families are likely to have more illnesses than those in non-manual social class families; the *General Household Survey* shows that children aged 0–15 with a father in Social Class V have 1.85 times the rate of limiting long-standing illness than those in Social Class I;
- children's development in terms of birthweight and height at primary school age is worse in deprived areas.[60]

The Health of our Children, Decennial Supplement, suggests there is some evidence that children's psychological health may be indirectly related to socio-economic conditions – for example, behavioural difficulties are more associated with children in poorer social groups. Studies have shown that 7 per cent of inner city three-year-olds were affected by moderate or severe behavioural difficulties.[61]

HOMELESSNESS

Homelessness is the most extreme aspect of poor housing conditions. Living in damp, draughty homes, waiting for repairs, being over-crowded, are all ways in which poverty directly impinges on people's lives.

> London has a shanty town as large as might be expected in a Latin American city, but it is hidden. People live illegally in squats or in cramped, badly equipped hotels and crowded hostels. If they do not fall into a group that the government recognises as having a special need, or they cannot locate one of the very few spare spaces indoors, they find they have no choice but to survive on the streets.[62]

The *Households below Average Income* and the *Low Income Families* statistics cover only private households and therefore do not include people who are living in hostels, bed and breakfast hotels, or out on the streets. It is a perverse irony that the available statistics on poverty exclude the very poorest.

NUMBERS OF HOMELESS PEOPLE

The growth of homelessness over the 1980s and 1990s has been dramatic. However, measuring the extent of homelessness is fraught with difficulties of definition. The Department of the Environment publishes quarterly statistics on the number of 'official homeless' – ie, those households which have been accepted by local authorities as being in 'priority need' and who are not intentionally homeless under the Housing Act 1985 (Part III).[63] (Priority need is defined as families with children, pregnant women, or those made vulnerable through old age, disability or other reasons.) However, the number of 'unofficial homeless' is much harder to estimate. The figures presented below are for England unless otherwise stated:

- In 1994, 122,660 households (containing 69,290 households with children) were accepted as homeless by local authorities. This is a fall from the peak in 1991, when the figure stood at 144,780, but remains a substantial rise since 1979, when 55,530 households fell into this category.[64]
- Despite the fall in the number of 'official homeless', there is a growing gap between the number of applications and acceptances by local authorities. In the third quarter of 1995 total applications amounted to over 85,200, while acceptances stood at 31,530 for the same period.[65]
- Homelessness is particularly acute in London – in 1994, 9.8 in every 1,000 households were accepted as homeless compared to 6.2 in England as a whole.[66]
- In 1995, local authorities were housing 46,160 households in temporary accommodation. (These households were either waiting for further enquiries or for permanent accommodation.) While this is a fall from the peak in 1992 – 65,500 – the trend shows a sharp rise since 1980, when households in temporary accommodation stood at just 4,710.[67]
- In 1995 the total of 46,160 households in temporary accommodation was broken down as follows: 5,270 (11 per cent) were in bed and breakfast hotels; 10,540 (23 per cent) were in hostels or women's refuges; 12,100 (26 per cent) were in the private sector, and 40 per cent were in other kinds of accommodation.[68]
- Local authority use of bed and breakfast hotels has declined. However, in a recent report, *Out of Sight … London's continuing B&B crisis*,[69] Mary Carter suggests that growing numbers of homeless people, who fall outside the scope of local authority

responsibility, are placing themselves in hotels. Thus, local authority figures of placements in temporary accommodation provide only a partial picture of the extent of the problem.

• The 'unofficial homeless' comprise a range of different groups such as those people who fall outside the category of 'priority need', in particular single people and couples without children, people sleeping rough, people who have to share with friends or relatives but need a home of their own. There is no *overall* estimate of the 'unofficial homeless', largely because of problems of definition.

• According to the 1991 Census, 2,674 people were sleeping rough. However, this figure is generally regarded as a substantial under-estimate – many rough sleepers are not easily visible (for example, sleeping in sheds or barns), there are seasonal variations in the number sleeping rough and movement between temporary accommodation such as hostels and sleeping outside.[70]

• *Single Homeless People*, a survey by the Department of the Environment of around 2,000 single homeless people in hostels, bed and breakfast hotels and sleeping rough in 1993 found that:
  – the majority were men;
  – they were more likely to be under 25 years of age and less likely to be over 60 than the general population;
  – Black people and other minority ethnic groups were over-represented in temporary accommodation, especially women;
  – the most common source of income was income support, followed by asking for money from people in the street;
  – average weekly income was £39 for those in hostels, bed and breakfast and hostels and £37 among those at soup runs;
  – one in five sleeping rough said that they had no income in the previous week;
  – the majority, in particular those sleeping rough, reported health problems;
  – a substantial proportion had spent time with a foster parent, or in a children's home or institution or the armed forces.[71]

CAUSES OF HOMELESSNESS

The principal reason for homelessness is a shortage of rented housing at reasonable prices. However, there are a number of immediate reasons for becoming homeless: breakdown of sharing arrangements; dissolution of a marriage or other partnership; loss of a private rented tenancy, and other reasons such as mortgage default and rent arrears.[72] The changes in social security for young people have meant that they are now far more at risk of homelessness than in the past.[73]

Recent government policy, in particular the changes to housing benefit and some of the proposals contained in the White Paper, *Our Future Homes*, may well increase levels of homelessness:[74]

- In January 1996 the government introduced a series of changes to housing benefit in the private rented sector which include the setting of housing benefit below market rents and the restriction of exceptional hardship payments.
- The government is proposing to limit housing benefit for under 25s to the cost of a bedsitting room, restricting levels of benefit for many single people from October 1996.
- The housing White Paper, *Our Future Homes*, proposes a major overhaul of the homelessness legislation, among other changes. The local authority duty to provide permanent housing for the 'priority' homeless is to be changed to provide *temporary* accommodation only for 12 months. The aim is to encourage local authorities to have a common waiting list for all housing applicants rather than a separate allocation of housing for the homeless. The homelessness charity, Shelter, has argued that the policy is likely to create 'revolving door clients', where people return to the local authority when their tenancies run out, and short-term tenancies which will result in greater movement, thus damaging job and educational opportunities.[75]

THE IMPACT OF HOMELESSNESS

The security of a home is essential for health, a sense of well-being and access to services and employment. These basic needs are beyond the reach of homeless people. A number of studies of living conditions in temporary accommodation graphically illustrate this fact.

The London Homelessness Forum documented conditions in bed and breakfast hotels in 1993 and found that:

- 14 out of 15 cots did not meet the British Safety Association standards;
- 95 per cent of families had no lockable storage space in their rooms;
- 30 per cent of families reported vermin in their rooms;
- 97 per cent of bedrooms did not have safety covers for electric sockets;

- 75 per cent of families had not had fire procedures explained to them;
- 50 per cent of families did not know where the fire exits were;
- 90 per cent of families said there was no safe play area for children.[76]

> A woman and her two children were staying in what was euphemistically termed a 'chalet'. In fact this was a flimsy temporary construction which had the benefit of only one solid wall – indeed one whole side of the room which included the 'front door' was predominantly glass. Condensation streamed down and the room had a cold, wet atmosphere. The heating was turned off during the day and because the bed would only fit in when pushed against the radiator, the family were stifled by heat at night and had to turn it off. The young boy had an almost constant cold since they moved in ... and has become unmanageable. His mother suffers from asthma and bronchitis.
> (Quoted in M Carter, *Out of Sight ... London's continuing B&B crisis*)[77]

Mary Carter found that the conditions in bed and breakfast hotels in 1995 were very similar to those in earlier studies in the 1980s: standards of safety were poor, space was limited, kitchen facilities inadequate, difficulties were encountered with heating and hot water, some rooms were infested and in some cases clients had not been treated well by hotel staff:

> Those who found the conditions most intolerable were families who faced the extra demands imposed upon them by small children. These are neither new nor surprising issues. Cramped single rooms which double up as kitchen, bedroom and living room, lack of parental privacy, difficulties in keeping children amused. All these combine to place families under immense stress.[78]

A high proportion of homeless families in temporary accommodation are now placed in private sector leased accommodation (PSL). A recent report by Rosalind Edwards and Jonathan Tritter for the London Homelessness Forum looked at the experiences of 56 homeless families.[79] They found that the families experienced a number of difficulties: they had to move with very little notice, with no time to make arrangements for changes of school or doctor; they had little knowledge of the area that they were moving into and did not know how long they would be there; some reported poor housing conditions and overcrowding. Aside from the practical difficulties of gaining access to schools and doctors in a new area:

Most of the families also had to travel some distance to gain access to the support networks they had previously built up – including family, friends and voluntary agencies. The expense and difficulty this entailed meant that, unless contact could be maintained by telephone, such support networks were often curtailed. Some of the mothers and fathers had difficulty in making new friendships in the neighbourhood of their PSL accommodation because of language, ethnic and other social barriers, as well as the attitudes of others to their homelessness and their own feelings of transience.[80]

Children who are homeless move around more and all children, when they come into school, need time to settle and find their feet before they start on the development of basic skills. The more schools a child attends, the more time is spent settling into school and that is education time lost.

(Head teacher, quoted in S Power *et al, No Place to Learn, homelessness and education*)[81]

In *No Place to Learn*, Shelter has documented the severe effects of homelessness on homeless children's education:

- 86 per cent of head teachers reported that homelessness had an impact on academic progress;
- parents had to face hard choices as to whether to keep children at their existing school, with the resulting high transport costs and difficulty of access, or move them;
- parents faced difficulties in finding new school places and settling children in school; as a result children were more likely to spend time out of school or attend irregularly;
- educational progress was hindered by frequent changes of school and attendance difficulties;
- children found it hard to work at home given their housing conditions;
- children found it difficult to participate fully in the life of school given their living conditions and their own experiences.[82]

... the children don't seem to be able to concentrate on their homework in this single room ... the children have to take in turns to do their homework at the table.

(Quoted in S Power *et al, No Place to Learn, homelessness and education*)[83]

CONCLUSION

Poverty casts a long shadow. It mars every aspect of life – meeting basic needs, joining in social activities, access to services and the chance of good health. We have looked at just four different aspects of poverty – living on benefits, coping with debts, experiencing poor health and being without a home. Obviously there are many other facets to the problem – poor housing, inadequate education, an environment that is dirty, noisy or dangerous, and patchy transport facilities. Not all of these are experienced by all those in poverty or only by those in poverty; yet there is no doubt that people in poverty are much more likely to suffer each of these forms of deprivation, and often multiple deprivation, than people who are better off. Each of these topics deserves a book in its own right (and many have been written). However, the evidence presented here highlights the hardship and anguish experienced by people living in poverty. It shows how poverty means going short of the basics; it means not being able to turn the heating on, or replace household goods, and not being able to go out. Poverty carries with it the risk of debt and the risk of homelessness. Above all, poverty puts at risk that most precious thing: the chance of a healthy and long life.

NOTES

1. P Golding (ed), *Excluding the Poor*, CPAG, 1986.
2. B Campbell, 'Poverty Demobilises', interview in *New Times*, 31 October 1992; and B Holman, 'Poverty is first among crimes', *Guardian*, 24 June 1992.
3. This chapter draws heavily on C Oppenheim and R Lister, 'Poverty and family life' in C Itzin (ed), *Home Truths*, Routledge, forthcoming.
4. L Morris and J Ritchie, *Income Maintenance and Living Standards*, SCPR and Joseph Rowntree Foundation, 1994.
5. E Kempson, A Bryson and K Rowlingson, *Hard Times*, Policy Studies Institute, 1994.
6. *See* note 5.
7. *See* note 5.
8. *See* note 5.
9. National Children's Home, *Poverty and Nutrition Survey*, 1991.
10. R Cohen, J Coxall, G Craig and A Sadiq-Sangster, *Hardship Britain, being poor in the 1990s*, CPAG Ltd in association with FSU, 1992.
11. *See* note 10.
12. *See* note 5.

13. *Family Spending. A report on the 1994–95 Family Expenditure Survey*, HMSO, 1995.
14. OPCS, *The Health of our Children, Decennial Supplement*, HMSO, 1995.
15. *See* note 10.
16. S Middleton, K Ashworth and R Walker, *Family Fortunes? Pressures on parents and children in the 1990s*, CPAG Ltd, 1994.
17. *See* note 14.
18. S Holtermann, *All Our Futures: the impact of public expenditure and fiscal policies on children and young people*, Barnardos, 1995. Two other important studies in this area are: V Kumar, *Poverty and Inequality in the UK: the effects on children*, National Children's Bureau, 1993; and R Wilkinson, *Unfair Shares: the effects of widening income differences on the welfare of the young*, Barnardos, 1994.
19. *See* Holtermann, note 18.
20. D Utting, *Family and Parenthood: Supporting families, preventing breakdown*, Joseph Rowntree Foundation, 1995.
21. *See* note 10.
22. *See* note 10.
23. Towerwatch, *Shame about the Service*, Archway Claimants' Action Group with Islington Council, 1992.
24. *See* note 10.
25. J Ford, *Consuming Credit: Debt and poverty in the UK*, CPAG Ltd, 1991.
26. J Ford, *Which Way Out? Borrowers with long-term mortgage arrears*, Shelter, 1995.
27. *See* note 26.
28. J Ford and S Wilcox, *Reducing Mortgage Arrears and Possessions: an evaluation of the initiatives*, Joseph Rowntree Foundation, 1992.
29. OFWAT, Press Release, 11 May 1995, and OFWAT, Press Release, 16 November 1992.
30. OFFER, *Customer Accounting Statistics ending September 1992*; OFFER, *Customer Accounting Statistics ending September 1995*; Gas Consumer Council, *Debt and Disconnecting Figures*, 1993; and Gas Consumer Council, *Annual Report*, 1994.
31. A Hoffland and N Nicol, *Fuel Rights Handbook*, CPAG Ltd, 1992.
32. NACAB, *Make or Break? CAB evidence on deductions from benefit*, 1993.
33. House of Commons, *Hansard*, 20 November 1995, cols 30–31.
34. *See* note 32.
35. *See* note 32.
36. R Mannion, S Hutton and R Sainsbury, *DSS Research Report No. 33, Direct Payments from Income Support*, HMSO, 1994.
37. R Berthoud and E Kempson, *Credit and Debt in Britain, The PSI Report*, PSI, 1992.
38. *See* note 37.
39. *See* note 5.

40. *See* note 5.
41. *See* note 4.
42. *See* note 4.
43. *See* note 25.
44. *See* note 4.
45. National Children's Home, *Deep in Debt: a survey of problems faced by low income families*, 1992.
46. *See* note 25.
47. M Benzeval, K Judge and M Whitehead (eds), *Tackling Inequalities in Health: an agenda for action*, Kings Fund, 1995.
48. OPCS, *Mortality Statistics, Perinatal and Infant: social and biological factors, 1978/79* and *1992*, HMSO, 1982 and 1995.
49. *The Health of the Nation, variations in health. What can the Department of Health and the NHS do?*, Department of Health, 1995; and M Benzeval et al, *see* note 47.
50. R Smith, 'Poor Britain: losing out', *British Medical Journal*, Vol 305, 1 August 1992.
51. R Smith, 'Unemployment: here we go again', *British Medical Journal*, vol 302, 16 March 1991.
52. *See* notes 50 and 51 and *Independent*, 27 January 1993.
53. *Nursing Times*, Vol 90, No 30, 27 July 1994.
54. B Graetz, 'Health consequences of employment and unemployment: longitudinal evidence for young men and women', *Social Science Medicine*, Vol 35, No 6, pp715–724, 1993; and M G Marmot et al, 'Health Inequalities among British Civil Servants: The Whitehall II Study', *Lancet*, Vol 337, pp1387–93, 1991, cited in *The Health of the Nation, variations in health, What can the Department of Health and the NHS do?*, Department of Health, 1995.
55. *See* note 4.
56. *General Household Survey 1993*, HMSO, 1995.
57. G Davy Smith, M Bartly and D Blane, 'The Black Report on socioeconomic inequalities in health: 10 years on', *British Medical Journal*, Vol 301, 18-25 August 1990.
58. *See* note 10.
59. *See* note 10.
60. *See* note 18.
61. *See* note 14.
62. D Canter et al, *The Faces of Homelessness in London: interim report to the Salvation Army*, January 1990.
63. Department of the Environment, *Information Bulletin*, 11 December 1995.
64. *See* note 63 and J Newton, *All in One Place*, CHAS, 1994.
65. *See* note 63.
66. *See* note 63.

67. *See* note 63 and J Newton, *All in One Place*, CHAS, 1994.
68. *See* note 63.
69. M Carter, *Out of Sight ... London's continuing B&B crisis*, CHAR, Shelter *et al*, 1995.
70. M Carter, *Extending the rough sleepers initiative: will the London model work?*, report commissioned jointly by Crisis and CHAR, 1995.
71. I Anderson, P Kemp and D Quilgars, *Single Homeless People, a report for the Department of the Environment*, HMSO, 1993.
72. L Burrows and P Walenkowicz, *Homes Cost Less than Homelessness*, Shelter, 1992.
73. R Strathdee, *No Way Back: homeless sixteen- and seventeen-year-olds in the 1990s*, Centrepoint Soho, 1992.
74. N Kirk, *Opportunity, Choice and Housing Benefit: a system in conflict*, CHAR, January 1996.
75. *Shelter's Guide to the 1995 Housing White Paper*, Shelter, 1995.
76. London Homelessness Forum, 1993, p13 cited in M Carter, *Out of Sight ... London's continuing B&B crisis*, CHAR, Shelter, *et al*, 1995.
77. *See* note 69.
78. *See* note 69.
79. R Edwards and J Tritter, *The Experience of Homeless Families in Private Sector Leased Temporary Accommodation*, Social Sciences Research Centre, South Bank University, London Homlessness Forum, 1993.
80. *See* note 76.
81. S Power, G Whitty and D Youdell, *No Place to Learn, homelessness and education*, Shelter, 1995.
82. *See* note 81.
83. *See* note 81.

5 Women and poverty

The simple fact is that throughout the last century women have always been much poorer than men. At the start of this century 61 per cent of adults on all forms of poor relief were women.

(*Women and Poverty in Britain*)[1]

There is nothing new about women's poverty. Today, 59 per cent of adults supported by income support are women.[2]

Focusing on women's poverty raises crucial issues for the examination of poverty as a whole.[3] Caroline Glendinning and Jane Millar's *Women and Poverty in Britain* brought together many of the central aspects of women's poverty. The authors argue that looking at women's risk of poverty is not simply a question of illuminating the disparate *levels* of income which exist between men and women. It is also about:

- their *access* to incomes and other resources; *and*
- the *time* spent in generating income and resources; *and*
- the *transfer* of these resources from some members of a household to others.

This approach facilitates a much more complete understanding of the nature of poverty which is not captured by straightforward statistics on family or household incomes.

INDICATORS OF WOMEN'S POVERTY

LOW INCOME

The major sources of data on poverty are not broken down by sex.

Income is measured by the household or family unit. The *Low Income Families Statistics* and the Department of Social Security's figures – *Households below Average Income* – are no exception. However, it is possible to make a rough estimate of how many women are living on benefit by making assumptions about the number of women who are lone parents, pensioners and so forth:[4]

• In 1992, approximately 5.4 million women and 4.2 million men were living in poverty (defined as on and below the income support level).

As the figures show, there are considerably more women in poverty than men – women outnumber men by about 1.2 million and make up around 56 per cent of the adults living in poverty. In an analysis of women's incomes, Steven Webb found that in 1991 around two-thirds of adults in the poorest households were women and women in these households had about half as much independent income as men – £99.90 per week compared with £199.50 (see Table 5.1).[5] The sources of income for men and women were noticeably different – eg, social security was the principal source of income for lone mothers and women pensioners. Not surprisingly, access to independent income from the labour market was associated with not having dependent children. Among married women, the amount of independent income was dependent on the age of the youngest child and the economic activity of the spouse.

TABLE 5.1: **Mean independent income of women, 1991, by source and by family type**

	Non-pensioners				Pensioners		
Income source (£ per week)	Single with children	Married with children	Single no children	Married no children	Single	Married	All women
Earnings	37.00	54.70	92.40	90.60	4.20	6.10	53.40
Self-employment	4.70	5.10	2.70	7.10	0.20	0.40	3.80
Social security	61.50	16.40	12.20	3.50	57.40	30.40	23.40
Investments	2.80	5.00	6.70	13.10	18.90	18.20	11.00
Pensions/annuities	2.60	0.20	2.10	1.50	19.70	6.50	4.90
Other	15.20	3.80	4.10	3.40	0.80	0.60	3.40
Total	**123.80**	**85.10**	**120.00**	**119.10**	**101.20**	**62.20**	**99.90**

Source: S Webb, 'Women's incomes: past, present and prospects', *Fiscal Studies*, Vol 14, no 4, Institute for Fiscal Studies, 1993.

UNEMPLOYMENT

> I have missed working. I've missed the company as much as the
> money. Before, I loved being at home but I loved being in work too
> and I miss it, the girls and all. I haven't really settled to it because my
> nerves have gone all wonky being in the house. It's all right when
> the children are here but when everybody goes I am back on my
> own all day.
>
> (Quoted in C Callender, *Redundancy, unemployment and poverty*)[6]

Because the official unemployment statistics are based on the numbers
claiming benefit or contribution credits, the full extent of
unemployment among women is hidden. The *Labour Force Survey*
count of unemployment shows much higher rates of unemployment
amongst women than the claimant count. In autumn 1994:

- 576,400 women were unemployed according to the claimant
  count – 24 per cent of all unemployed men and women;
- 846,800 women were unemployed according to the *Labour Force
  Survey* definition (ie, people who did no paid work in the previous week, had actively looked for work in the last four weeks
  and were free to start work in two weeks, regardless of whether
  they were claiming benefits) – 34 per cent of the total;
- in addition, 620,600 women were unemployed according to a
  slightly less stringent definition of unemployment in the *Labour
  Force Survey* (ie, people who want work, are available, but have not
  looked in the last four weeks) – 63 per cent of the total;
- 1,467,400 women were unemployed if you combine the two
  previous measures (ie, all wanting and available for work) – 43 per
  cent of the total.[7]

In financial terms redundancy is likely to be even worse for women
than men. Redundancy payments are based on length of service and
pay levels. Part-time workers are disadvantaged in terms of redundancy
pay. As Claire Callender writes:

> Women receive lower redundancy payments than men and a larger
> proportion of them are ineligible for payments altogether. This
> makes women cheaper to dismiss and makes them more vulnerable
> to redundancy.[8]

However, recent research from the Department of Employment
throws up contrary evidence; it shows that in 1992 women were less
likely to be made redundant and were also more likely to receive a

redundancy payment.[9] It is possible that changes in women's position in the labour market may account for these findings; however, the issue needs to be explored further.

LOW PAY

> I was earning roughly £35 to £40 a week. It was piece work, 13p per skirt – you had to sew hundreds to get to £35–£40...I had to work sometimes until midnight, from nine in the morning, just to pay rent, electricity and gas.
>
> (Sevin, mother of three)[10]

- In 1994, 6.41 million women were low paid – ie, 64 per cent of the total number of people on low wages according to the Council of Europe's decency threshold. (This was defined as £221.50 a week or £5.88 an hour in 1994.)
- There is a strong association between low pay and part-time work. In 1994, 4.83 million women worked part-time and 77 per cent of them were low paid. Only 1.11 million men worked part-time, with a slightly lower proportion who were low paid (72 per cent).[11]
- Many Black women are likely to have even lower earnings and/or do more shift work (see Chapter 6).
- In 1994, women's full-time gross weekly pay was 72 per cent of men's. Although this gap is still large, it has been narrowing since the introduction of equal pay and anti-discrimination legislation in the 1970s. In 1979 women's full-time gross weekly pay was 64 per cent of men's.[12]
- Research by the Equal Opportunities Commission estimated that around three-quarters of employees covered by Wages Council agreements were women. The abolition of the Wages Councils is likely to have a particularly detrimental effect on women's wages.

LONE MOTHERS

> It is precisely because lone mothers are women that they have a very high risk of poverty.
>
> (J Millar, *Lone Mothers and Poverty*)[13]

In 1992, there were 1.4 million lone mothers. Nine out of ten lone parents are women. As we have seen, they are much more likely to be in poverty than other groups:

- lone mothers' employment rates have declined in the last 10 years: according to the *General Household Survey*, in 1979-81, 49 per cent of lone mothers were in employment; in 1991-93 this had fallen to 41 per cent. By contrast, married mothers' employment rates increased over the same period from 52 per cent to 63 per cent.[14] Department of Employment data show that in 1993/94, 39 per cent of lone mothers with a child aged 0–15 were in employment compared to 62 per cent of women in married/cohabiting couples.[15] However, the government quotes research undertaken by the Policy Studies Institute which suggests that the *economic activity* rate of *lone parents* has risen since 1991.[16]
- 1,097,000 lone parents were reliant on income support in 1994. Well over half of lone parents were on income support for several years; 658,000 had been on supplementary benefit/income support for two years or more.[17] Being on benefit for long periods inevitably brings hardship and often debt.

The combination of coping with bringing up children on their own, the difficulties of managing on a single wage, very often at low levels, with little access to affordable childcare, means that many lone mothers find themselves forced to rely on means-tested benefits for long periods.

BENEFITS

Women are ... less likely than men to be receiving the superior contributory benefits and more likely to be receiving the inferior non-contributory equivalents. Many women are entitled to neither (leaving aside benefits for children) and are therefore reliant on means-tested income support or on a man for economic support.

(R Lister, *Women's Economic Dependency and Social Security*)[18]

One of the main features of our social security system is the division between national insurance benefits, non-contributory and means-tested benefits. As long as sufficient contributions have been made, national insurance benefits are paid on an individual basis regardless of income. Non-contributory benefits are not means-tested, but they are lower than national insurance benefits. Means-tested benefits are based on a test of income and capital. Because women are more likely to have breaks in employment and to work part time and earn low wages, many fall below the threshold for making national insurance contributions. In 1995-96, over 2.3 million women fell into this category.[19] The result is that women forfeit their right to national insurance benefits. Women are therefore less likely to have benefits in their own right than men, and as a result are more dependent on non-contributory benefits and the 'Cinderella' part of the social security system – means-tested benefits.

Table 5.2 below, updated from Ruth Lister's research for the EOC, illustrates this clearly.[20] More men are claiming contributory benefits for people below pension age and more women are claiming means-tested and non-contributory benefits. Retirement pension (a contributory benefit) is an exception to this pattern because of the high proportion of women pensioners. However, a much higher proportion of women over pension age are reliant on income support than men over pension age. In 1994, 18 per cent of women over pension age (1,195,000) claimed income support compared to 6 per cent of men (206,000).[21]

TABLE 5.2: **Percentage of social security claimants by sex, 1993/94**

Great Britain		per cent
Benefit	Men	Women
Industrial injury disablement benefit	86	14
Invalidity benefit	73	27
Maternity benefit	nil	100
Non-contributory retirement pension	20	80
Retirement pension	35	65
Sickness benefit	58	42
Unemployment benefit	76	24
Widow's benefit	nil	100
Reduced earnings allowance	81	19
Attendance allowance	29	71
Child benefit	3	97
One-parent benefit	9	91
Invalid care allowance	31	69
Mobility allowance	52	48
Severe disablement allowance	38	62
Family credit[1]	43	57
Income support	48	52
Disability living allowance	52	48
Disability working allowance	60	40

Note: 1. Figures based on sex of main earner.

Source: House of Commons, *Hansard*, 25 May 1995, cols 695-7

EXCLUSION

The indicators of poverty so far look at hard facts, like wages and social security. But there are less quantifiable aspects to poverty, like not being able to go out for a drink or a meal, or missing out on seeing friends. There is some evidence to show that this aspect of poverty is also different for women and men. A local poverty survey undertaken in Islington in 1990 looked at social deprivation. This was defined as lack of rights in employment, such as no paid holiday or sick pay; lack of activities for children; lack of integration into the community, such as being lonely and cut off; not voting; and lack of education. The survey found that 37 per cent of women experienced severe social deprivation compared with 30 per cent of men.[22] This bears out earlier findings from a survey of 140 families living on supplementary benefit in Tyne and Wear which compared activities pursued outside the home by women and men on benefit. While living on benefit severely curtailed the activities of both sexes, women, on the whole, were even less likely to participate in such activities:

- 18 per cent of men went out for a drink compared to 3 per cent of women;
- 18 per cent of men took part in sport compared to 8 per cent of women;
- 11 per cent of men went to the unemployed workers' centre while no women did.

On the other hand, women were far more likely to be cooking the main meal or cleaning and dusting.[23]

THE CAUSES OF WOMEN'S POVERTY

Many women's lives are still shaped by the family responsibilities they have traditionally been expected to take on – the tasks of childcare, caring for the elderly and maintaining the home. These tasks shape women's work patterns, the type of occupations they work in, their earnings and their social security benefits. They push women into financial dependence upon men or upon state benefits. It is often assumed that women do not need an income of their own and that money, food and other resources are shared evenly within the family. For many women neither employment nor social security can keep them out of poverty.

WOMEN'S UNPAID WORK

DOMESTIC LABOUR

Women are responsible for the bulk of domestic work. *British Social Attitudes*, an annual survey, looked at the distribution of household tasks undertaken by women and men.[24] It found that the traditional division of labour is alive and kicking. In 1991:

- 45 per cent of women were mainly responsible for shopping compared to 8 per cent of men (47 per cent share);
- 70 per cent of women were mainly responsible for making the evening meal compared to 9 per cent of men (20 per cent share);
- 68 per cent of women were mainly responsible for cleaning compared to 4 per cent of men (27 per cent share);
- 84 per cent of women were mainly responsible for washing and ironing compared to 3 per cent of men (12 per cent share);
- 60 per cent of women looked after children when sick compared to 1 per cent of men (39 per cent share).

The only household task that men were more likely to do than women was repairing household equipment – 82 per cent of men were mainly responsible for this task compared to 6 per cent of women.

Married women are less likely to work full time than those women without a partner. Heather Joshi argues that:

> the lower propensity of married women to take full-time jobs even when they have no young children must ... partly arise from the extra demands on their time of looking after husband, home and social network.[25]

The European Commission Network on Childcare has recently found that fathers with a child under 10 in the UK work on average 47 hours a week – the longest in the European Union.[26] In her study of men and women's working hours for the Equal Opportunities Commission, Catherine Marsh found that the usual pattern was that one partner (usually male) worked very long hours and the other (usually female) worked much shorter hours and thus there was 'very little evidence of domestic job sharing'.[27] She concludes:

> There seems no way in which a style of work which involved such a long commitment to paid employment could be emulated by anyone who had a major responsiblity for children. It might be useful to

consider regulation of the hours of work of men as the single most effective means of promoting equality at the workplace.

Marsh's findings are confirmed by more recent research conducted in the UK by Alan Marsh and Stephen McKay. In an analysis of over 9,000 people, it found full-time women workers worked an average of 35 hours per week compared to 43 hours among full-time men.[28]

This division of labour within the home reflects the more traditional attitudes of men towards women's domestic responsibilities than the views of women themselves. Sharon Witherspoon and Gillian Prior found that just over one half of fathers disagreed with the view that the man should be the main breadwinner and the woman should look after the home and children, compared to three-quarters of women. They conclude:

> Whatever talk there is of the 'New Man', he is much rarer than the 'New Woman'. This gap in attitudes has consequences for family life in general, as well as for women's decisions to work outside the home. In the absence of changes in men's attitudes, or in their working hours outside the home, or in their contribution within the family towards childcare and domestic duties, it seems unlikely that even a greater availability of childcare outside the home would alter domestic arrangements greatly. Indeed without these changes, it is conceivable that many useful forms of work flexibility which might be offered to women – such as job-sharing, career-breaks, special sick-leave, or term-time working – might serve to reinforce rather than mitigate the already formidable level of occupational segregation based on gender, to women's longer term disadvantage.[29]

The European Community Working Hours Directive, which sets maximum daily, weekly and night hours as well as minimum annual leave (with some exceptions), will come into force in November 1996 but, as a result of UK opposition to the draft Directive, it has been watered down.

CARING FOR CHILDREN

Looking after children swallows up a large amount of time and is still usually done by women. A 1984 survey estimated that women with a child under five were spending an average of 50 hours a week on basic childcare tasks.[30] More recently, the *London Living Standards Survey* found that among parents with a child under five, women spent 65 hours a week on childcare compared to 20 hours spent by men.[31]

Caring for children has a knock-on effect on women's employment and earning capacity. Heather Joshi compared the average earnings of a woman with two children to that of a woman with none over their lifetimes. She found that a mother with two children would lose an average of £202,500 in foregone earnings over a lifetime.[32] This is the result of eight years out of the labour market, working part-time and having lower earnings. This takes no account of the loss of pension rights. Joshi estimates that these may amount to as much as the overall loss in earnings. Joshi also compared the lifetime average earnings of a woman without children with a man and found that the difference was nearly as much as the difference between a woman with no children and a mother. Thus, simply being female has a downward pressure on overall earnings.[33]

CARING FOR ELDERLY OR SICK OR DISABLED PEOPLE

I hadn't anticipated giving up work, I thought I could manage the three hours. But the thing was ... in the summer days she came out to meet me, her petticoat round her top. She'd got changed during the afternoon. My heart nearly broke when I saw her ... and then twice she ran after me as I was getting on the bus – didn't want me to go. The time had come to stop work.

(Ms Grey, who gave up her job as a child welfare clinic clerical officer several months after her mother came to live with her, quoted in C Glendinning, *The Costs of Informal Care*)[34]

It is not only caring for children that has a knock-on effect on women's lost earnings, but also caring for adult relatives who are elderly or sick or have a disability. There has been a great deal of discussion about the overall number of carers and what proportion of those are women. The British Household Panel Study examined informal caring. It found that in 1991:

- almost one in seven adults provided informal care either inside or outside their home;
- 17 per cent of women and 12 per cent of men were informal carers;
- women spent more time than men caring: 41 per cent of women spent over 50 hours a week caring for someone living with them compared to 28 per cent of men;

- caring had a marked impact on employment patterns: 43 per cent of married women carers of working age were also in employment compared to 60 per cent of married women as a whole; 62 per cent of male carers were also in employment compared to 77 per cent of men as a whole.[35]

The *financial cost* of caring is substantial. Maria Evandrou has shown that female sole carers have a slightly greater risk of having less money than male sole carers: 23 per cent of female sole carers fell into the bottom fifth of the income distribution, compared to 20 per cent of men.[36] Heather Joshi has estimated that in 1990 the annual 'cost' of giving up full-time work in the later stages of life to care for an elderly or sick person was £12,750 for someone without children and £10,500 for a mother. (The losses are lower for women with children because their earnings have already been depressed by having children.)[37]

TIME COSTS

Work at home, whether caring for the home or children or adults, is often neglected in any discussion of poverty. The amount of *time* spent trying to achieve a given standard of living − eg, cleaning, cooking and other forms of 'home production' − is an important aspect of poverty.[38] Jane Millar and Caroline Glendinning argue:

> The value of time − both in the generation of resources and in their use − has hitherto been largely ignored in poverty studies. If time were included it would almost certainly point out substantial differences between men and women.[39]

In other words, poverty is not just about income but about how income and other resources are generated and used. For example, it may take a woman on low pay 50 hours a week to earn an average wage while a woman on higher earnings might need to work half as many hours to achieve the same income. The amount of *time* trying to earn a living wage is an important aspect of her poverty. Another example is the amount of time it takes to do household tasks. Visits to the launderette, daily trips to the shops because there is never enough money for a big shop, making sandwiches because there isn't enough money for school dinners − all these absorb time. Not having sufficient money, or a washing machine, or a car, all mean that it takes much more time and work for someone in poverty to achieve the same standard of living as someone who is comfortably off.

WOMEN'S PAID WORK

On the whole, women still work in particular parts of the job market – the sexual division of labour remains entrenched. The latest *Labour Force Survey* in 1995 shows that nearly 70 per cent of working women were employed in non-manual work (compared to half of men) and that 85 per cent worked in service industries (compared with 59 per cent of men).[40]

The division between women and men in the world of paid work reflects the division of labour in the home. In 1995:

• 25 per cent of women in employment worked in clerical occupations compared to 7 per cent of men;
• 16 per cent of women in employment worked in personal and protective services, such as catering, cleaning and hairdressing, compared to 7 per cent of men;
• 11 per cent of women in employment worked in selling compared to 5 per cent of men.[41]

Many of these occupations have high proportions of low-paid workers. According to the *New Earnings Survey*, in 1995:

• 52 per cent of women full-timers in clerical and secretarial occupations earned below £220 a week; there were much higher proportions of women earning below this level in particular occupations in this sector: 65 per cent of other secretaries, 84 per cent of receptionists/telephonists and 69 per cent of library assistants/clerks earned below this level;
• 72 per cent of women full-timers in personal and protective services earned below £220 a week; within this sector 96 per cent of waitresses, 90 per cent of hairdresser and related occupations and 86 per cent of childcare-related occupations earned below this level;
• 73 per cent of women full-timers who worked in sales occupations earned below £220 a week; within this sector 92 per cent of retail cash desk and checkout operators earned below this level.[42]

Although occupational segregation between men and women remains entrenched, recent labour market trends have changed the nature of that segregation. In an analysis of occupational change, R A Wilson shows how women's share of employment has increased in nearly all occupations and will continue to do so in future years.[43] Women's growing participation in the labour market is in part triggered by the growth of the service sector and the continuing decline of manual jobs. However, Wilson shows how the new jobs have been and will continue to be predominantly part time and that the growth of self-employment will persist. While women's employment prospects are likely to remain positive, Wilson also argues that:

> Women are also likely to remain highly segregated in occupational employment terms, with a few occupations continuing to provide most 'women's' jobs. Even where women are increasing their shares of employment in higher level occupations, there remains a danger that such broad occupational categories conceal further patterns of segregation.[44]

Women have had far less access to occupational and fringe benefits at work. A study found that in 1989 a lower proportion of full-time women workers had access to almost all types of benefit (after allowing for differences in skill and job content) in comparison with men. For part-time women workers this pattern was even more marked (see Table 5.3).[45] However, as a result of a ruling by the European Court, the government has now legislated to end sex discrimination in company pension schemes. Part-time women workers must now be given access to occupational pension schemes on an equal basis to men.[46]

Women are far more likely to be working part time than men because of their domestic responsibilities. The 1994 *Labour Force Survey* showed that:

- 64.5 per cent of full-time employees were men and 35.5 per cent were women;
- 15 per cent of part-time employees were men and 85 per cent were women.[47]

> A CAB in the West Midlands reported a client who was a single parent with one child, who applied for a job. The next day she was informed, 'you were clearly the best candidate but we are not giving you the job because of your son; we don't think you'll be able to cope.'[48]

Patterns of part-time work are directly linked to responsibilities for caring for children or others. As the youngest child gets older the mother is more likely to be in paid work. A majority of women with children in the youngest age group are not in paid work (see Table 5.4).

TABLE 5.3: **Percentage of jobs where employer provides benefits, by gender**

	Male full-timers	Female full-timers	Female part-timers
pensions*	73	68	31
sick pay*	66	58	27
paid time off	64	48	30
unpaid time off	54	54	57
company car or van	30	10	5
free/subsidised transport	31	24	17
goods at a discount	47	40	31
free or subsidised meals	39	47	25
finance/loans	21	20	12
accommodation	14	17	5
life assurance	39	19	5
private health	31	22	9
recreation facilities	40	36	24
maternity pay	n/a	31	16
childcare	1	13	10

*above basic government scheme
Source: *Unequal Jobs, Unequal Pay*, ESRC, The Social Change and Economic Life Initiative, Working Paper 6, 1989

TABLE 5.4: **Employment rates for women of working age with children in 1993/94**

	age of youngest child		
	0-4	5-10	11-15
% working full time	16.2	20.4	34.0
% working part time	30.0	45.1	40.3
% working	46.1	65.7	74.3

Note: Percentages in some cases do not add up due to rounding.

Source: Department of Employment, *Labour Force Survey* 1993/94

Getting paid work is also intimately linked to the availability of child care. The UK has the lowest level of publicly-funded childcare provision (2 per cent) for under-threes in the European Union. Sixty per cent of three- to six-year-olds have access to publicly-funded childcare in the UK. Compare this with 91 per cent in Italy and 99 per cent in France.[49]

> I don't want to leave her with a childminder, with the money I'd make, I'd lose ... I would be more in debt working than I would be on income support or the social, so I think 'No, I'm not going back to work ...' I would go back to work when she is in full-time school.
> (Melanie, mother of 21-month-old daughter)[50]

An important new development is the *decrease* in the number of hours worked by women with jobs. According to Catherine Marsh, in 1979, 29.8 per cent of female manual part-time workers and 23 per cent of female non-manual part-time workers worked less than 16 hours a week.[51] By 1995, this had risen to 48 per cent and 36 per cent respectively.[52] This trend is important because it means women are able to earn less money and are less likely to qualify for certain social security benefits. Until a ruling made by the House of Lords on 3 March 1994, part-time workers working less than 16 hours a week were also less likely to be covered by the employment protection legislation.[53] The House of Lords judgment now means that part-time workers (who have been employed continuously for two years) have effective rights to claim redundancy and unfair dismissal on the same basis as full-timers. Under the Trade Union Reform and Employment Rights Act, women have gained a right to protection from dismissal due to pregnancy and 14 weeks of maternity leave without qualifying conditions. There have therefore been some important changes which have gone some way to reducing the disadvantages faced by part-time workers (largely women) in terms of their employment rights.

The shift in industrial structure to service industries, the increase in part-time work, the decrease in the number of hours worked by women and the expansion of temporary work and Sunday working are all aspects of the 'flexible' labour market. A much higher proportion of women are part of the 'flexible' workforce (defined as all those who are not full-time permanent employees). In 1993, 38 per cent of all those in employment were in the flexible workforce, 27 per cent of men and 52 per cent of women. Although the proportion of men in this sector of the labour market has risen substantially since 1981, the proportion of women has stayed roughly the same.[54] The shift to a more flexible labour market has not always served women well; in Ruth Lister's words:

> ... at the very time women's economic activity rates are increasing, the labour market is decreasingly likely to offer them an adequate income.[55]

Despite the evidence that women are disadvantaged in the world of paid work in comparison with men, there is growing evidence that women's earnings are increasingly important to family income – they rose from 27 per cent to 35.6 per cent of household income between 1971 and 1991.[56] The importance of women's incomes in shielding families from economic misfortune is borne out by research by Machin and Waldfogel, who found that the rate of poverty among couples in 1990/91 would have been 50 per cent higher if women had not been earning.[57]

WHOSE MONEY?

> I don't treat myself a lot. It usually goes on [my daughter]. It's quite difficult because you know the way [kids are today], they like everything with names and it's quite difficult. I do the best I can for her.
> (Jacqui, quoted in E Kempson *et al*, *Hard Times?*
> *How poor families make ends meet*)[58]

The distribution of money, food and other goods inside the home is an area which is seen as *private* and is therefore very difficult to research.[59] The quotation above illustrates the ways in which women often put the needs of their families above their own. By impoverishing themselves, women help to prevent or reduce poverty for other members of their family.[60] Thus a woman can be in poverty while other members of her family are not or she may be in deeper poverty than they are. Research by Vogler in 1989 looked at 1,200 households. She found that only a fifth used a system of pooling money between husband and wife and that women 'command less of the family income than men'.[61] This confirms earlier research by Jan Pahl who looked at how money is handled inside the family.[62] She showed that women in couples are likely to have less income of their own than men: 83 per cent of women in couples had an income of less than £57 a week compared with 6 per cent of men (the result of differential earnings, savings, gifts and child benefit). Pahl also found that in poorer households and in households in the North, North-West and in Wales, women are more likely to be responsible for the family budget. But holding the purse strings does not necessarily confer power:

> Women are responsible for family finances but they have none of the power that goes with possession. Having it in their hands never made money their own.
>
> (Beatrix Campbell)[63]

Research by Elaine Kempson *et al* has shown that while women are less likely than men to control the budget, they are more likely to manage it.[64] This brings particular stresses and anxieties. The study of families on supplementary benefit in Tyne and Wear found that there were higher stress levels among women than men and that women's (but not men's) stress levels were associated with the level of debt in the family.[65]

The bulk of the money a woman brings into the home is spent on household consumption. Pahl found that, as far as household spending was concerned, men contributed more in absolute terms and women contributed more in relative terms:

> Put simply, if a pound entered the household economy through the mother's hands more of it would be spent on food for the family than would be the case if the pound had been brought into the household by the father.[66]

In addition, Pahl found that the men were more likely to have money for personal spending and leisure than the women:

- 44 per cent of men compared to 28 per cent of women had personal spending money;
- 86 per cent of men and 67 per cent of women spent money on leisure pursuits.[67]

> Well, his spending money was probably £150, which I felt was a bit unfair because I could never spend money on myself. But, yes, I was quite happy and I said nothing. But then it got to the stage that he wanted the bills being paid but then again he wanted extra at the end of the month when he has no money or when he spends it and I wasn't allowed to do that because I couldn't afford it.[68]

It is not only the sharing of money and resources that can be unequal within a home, but also the impact of things that a family does not have. For example, living in an overcrowded flat with damp and heating problems has a greater effect on a mother at home with a child than on her husband who is at work, simply because of the amount of time the woman spends at home.

> Not having hot water or a bathroom means different things to the man who uses hot water for washing and shaving in comparison with the woman who is responsible for childcare, the washing of clothes and cleaning the house.
>
> (S Payne, *Women, Health and Poverty*)[69]

FAILURES IN THE SOCIAL SECURITY SYSTEM

The social security system fails to protect women adequately from poverty because it does not recognise the complexity of most women's lives. Beveridge's social security scheme assumed a traditional family unit with a full-time male breadwinner and a woman at home looking after the home and children. The social security system has not kept pace with changes in women's roles and employment patterns. Such a model cannot accommodate the mixture of paid work and unpaid work (such as caring for children and others) and the changes in family patterns which particularly affect women's capacity to provide an adequate income for themselves and their families. Many of the recent changes in social security have had a detrimental effect on women. Here are just a few examples:[70]

- the abolition of the universal maternity grant. This has been replaced by the maternity payment now available only to women on income support and family credit, which has not kept pace with inflation; the DSS has tightened up guidance for issuing maternity payments: clothes for growing children and maternity clothes are discretionary rather than mandatory
- childcare costs cannot be offset against earnings for income support claimants (as they could under supplementary benefit);
- the introduction of the social fund with all its weaknesses (such as loans and budget limits) particularly affects women. Lone parents (most of whom are women) have a high reliance on the social fund. The difficulties of repaying loans and the effect of this on managing budgets very often falls on women's shoulders as they are more likely to have overall budgeting responsibility;
- the freezing of child benefit between 1988 and 1990 means that, despite recent increases, its real value has gone down since 1979;
- the abolition of free school meals for family credit recipients (although there was some cash compensation);

- the weakening of the state earnings related pension which is now based on a lifetime's earnings and only partially protects women with domestic responsibilities;
- the emphasis on private provision such as private pensions, which tends to reinforce market inequalities between men and women;
- the introduction of the Child Support Act has done little to improve the living standards of the poorest lone mothers and their children on income support;[71]
- the freezing of the lone parent premium and one-parent benefit announced in the 1995 Budget, as well as the in principle commitment to phase out extra help for lone parents in the social security system.

There have been some positive changes such as extra help for carers (there is a carers' premium in income support), increased earnings disregards for carers and lone parents and new benefits for people with disabilities. In particular, the introduction of an allowance of £40 (to be increased to £60 from April 1996) towards the cost of childcare for some groups receiving family credit and other benefits is a welcome, albeit limited, improvement.[72] However, as Ruth Lister concludes:

> the dominant trends in social security policy have been to place greater emphasis on means-tested as opposed to non-means-tested provision and on private as opposed to public forms of income maintenance. Whilst certain specific policies have been to women's advantage, the overall impact of these trends is corrosive of women's economic independence.[73]

CONCLUSION

Women's poverty is compounded over a lifetime. Their lower rates of pay, work patterns interrupted because of caring for others, the trap of part-time work, and the diminished social security, occupational and private benefits received as a result of their work patterns combine to impoverish women throughout their lives. Women's longer life expectancy and their reduced access to pensions mean that a high proportion are living out their lives on pitiful levels of income.

Many measures which would help people living in poverty would benefit women in particular. CPAG believes that the following policies would begin to deal with the poverty faced by women:

- A statutory minimum wage for full- and part-time workers and improved equal pay laws.
- Including part-time employees in sickness and maternity insurance schemes.
- Improving the rights of parents in employment (eg, parental leave, paternity and maternity leave, etc).
- Developing training schemes which encourage young women to work in occupations which are traditionally male and vice versa.
- The replacement of the national insurance threshold with a tax threshold so that employers and employees (largely women) no longer have an incentive to create, or work in, jobs of very few hours a week.
- Encouraging employers to extend flexible working arrangements such as flexible hours, job-sharing arrangements, working from home and term-time contracts for men as well as for women.
- Restoration of full rights of income support for pregnant 16-24-year-olds, a maternity premium in means-tested benefits and an increase in the social fund maternity payment. In the longer term, the reintroduction of a lump sum maternity payment for all pregnant women.
- Increased availability of subsidised childcare including school holiday care and care for after school hours.
- Disregarding childcare costs for those on income support.
- Steps towards a non-means-tested social security system without restrictive contribution conditions so that women with caring responsibilities would not be penalised for spending time out of the labour market.
- Individual entitlement to non-means-tested benefits.

NOTES

1. J Lewis and D Piachaud, 'Women and poverty in the twentieth century', in C Glendinning and J Millar (eds), *Women and Poverty in Britain, the 1990s*, Wheatsheaf, 1992.
2. This is based on the following assumptions: in 1994, 2,973,000 women and 2,702,000 men received income support, 992,000 partners were provided for, 97 per cent of whom were women. This makes a total of 3,935,240 women and 2,731,760 men provided for by income support. See DSS, *Social Security Statistics 1995*, Government Statistical Service, HMSO, 1995.

3. J Millar and C Glendinning, 'Gender and poverty: a survey article', *Journal of Social Policy*, Vol 18, Part 3, July 1989.
4. Using income support statistics this figure assumes that 32 per cent of single people (excluding lone parents) under pension age are women; that 85 per cent of single people over pension age are women; that 94 per cent of lone parents on income support are women. Figures derived from DSS, *Social Security Statistics* (*see* note 2).
5. S Webb, 'Women's incomes: past, present and prospects', *Fiscal Studies*, Vol 14, No 4, pp14-36, Institute for Fiscal Studies, 1993, cited in C Oppenheim and R Lister, 'Poverty and family life' in C Itzin (ed), *Home Truths*, Routledge, forthcoming.
6. C Callender, 'Redundancy, unemployment and poverty', in C Glendinning and J Millar (eds), *see* note 1.
7 Unemployment Unit, *Working Brief* 63, April 1995.
8. *See* note 6.
9. B Casey, *Redundancy in Britain – findings from the Labour Force Survey*, ED Research Brief No 62, 1995.
10. Quoted in 'Women and poverty' photographic exhibition, CPAG, 1986.
11. *The New Review*, No 30, Low Pay Unit, November/December 1994.
12. *See* note 10.
13. J Millar, 'Lone mothers and poverty', in C Glendinning and J Millar (eds), *see* note 1.
14. *General Household Survey 1993*, Table 5.9, HMSO, 1995.
15. Department of Employment, *Statistical Update, Employment Gazette*, January 1995, HMSO, 1995.
16. F Ford, A Marsh and S McKay, *Changes in Lone Parenthood*, Policy Studies Institute, 1995.
17. Department of Social Security, *Social Security Statistics 1994*, HMSO, 1995.
18. R Lister, *Women's Economic Dependency and Social Security*, Equal Opportunities Commission, 1992.
19. House of Commons, *Hansard*, 14 June 1995, col 516.
20. *See* note 18.
21. *See* note 17 and OPCS, *Population Trends, 81*, HMSO, Autumn 1995.
22. Islington Council, *Islington: Poverty in the 80s, A digest*, London Borough of Islington, 1990.
23. J Bradshaw and H Holmes, *Living on the Edge: a study of the living standards of families on benefit living in Tyne and Wear*, Tyneside CPAG, 1989.
24. K Kiernan, 'Men and women at work and at home', in R Jowell *et al* (eds), *British Social Attitudes, the 8th report, 1991/92*, SCPR, Dartmouth, 1991.
25. H Joshi, 'The cost of caring', in C Glendinning and J Millar (eds), *see* note 1.

26. *A Review of Childcare Services for Young Children in the European Union 1990–1995*, European Network on Childcare, Brussels, Equal Opportunities Unit, 1996.

27. C Marsh, *Hours of Work of Women and Men in Britain*, Equal Opportunities Commission, HMSO, 1991.

28. A Marsh and S McKay, 'Families, work and the use of childcare', *Employment Gazette, August 1993*, Department of Employment.

29. S Witherspoon and G Prior, 'Working mothers: free to choose', in R Jowell *et al* (eds), *see* note 24.

30. D Piachaud, *Round about 50 Hours a Week*, CPAG, 1984.

31. U Kowarzik and J Popay, *London Living Standards Survey, unpaid work*, unpublished paper, 1991.

32. *See* note 25.

33. *See* note 25.

34. C Glendinning, *The Costs of Informal Care: looking inside the household*, Social Policy Research Unit, HMSO, 1992.

35. L Corti and S Dex, 'Informal carers and employment', *Employment Gazette, March 1995*, Department of Employment, HMSO, 1995.

36. M Evandrou, *Challenging the Invisibility of Carers: mapping informal care nationally*, WSP/49, Suntory Toyota International Centre for Economics and Related Disciplines, 1990.

37. *See* note 25.

38. D Piachaud, 'Problems in the definition and measurement of poverty', *Journal of Social Policy*, Vol 116, Part 2, April 1987.

39. *See* note 1.

40. *Labour Force Survey Quarterly Bulletin*, No 14, Central Statistical Office, 1995.

41. *See* note 40.

42. Department of Employment, *New Earnings Survey 1995*, HMSO, 1995.

43. R A Wilson, 'Sectoral and occupational change: prospects for women's employment', in R Lindley (ed), *Labour Market Structures and Prospects for Women*, Equal Opportunities Commission, 1994.

44. *See* note 43.

45. S Howell, J Rubery, B Burchell, *Unequal Jobs, Unequal Pay*, Economic and Social Research Council, Working Paper 6, 1989.

46. DSS, Press Release 95/061, 10 May 1995.

47. Department for Education and Employment, *Employment Gazette, August 1995*, Labour Market Update Table 7.4, HMSO, 1995.

48. NACAB, *Unequal Opportunities, CAB evidence on discrimination in employment*, NACAB, 1994.

49. These figures should be interpreted with care; comprehensive data on European childcare services are not available. For a fuller discussion see *A Review of Services for Young Children in the European Union, 1990-*

1995, European Network on Childcare, Brussels, Equal Opportunities Unit, 1996.

50. E Kempson, A Bryson and K Rowlingson, *Hard Times? How poor families make ends meet*, Policy Studies Institute, 1994.

51. See note 27.

52. House of Commons, *Hansard*, 22 November 1995, col 191.

53. Equal Opportunities Commission, *Guidance on legal implications of House of Lords Judgment in R v Secretary of State for Employment: Ex Parte EOC*, 3 March 1994.

54. G Weston, 'The flexible workforce and patterns of working hours in the UK', *Employment Gazette, July 1994*, Department of Employment.

55. See note 18.

56. See note 5.

57. S Machin and J Waldfogel, 'The decline of the male breadwinner', *Welfare State Programme/103*, STICERD, 1994.

58. See note 50.

59. J Brannen and G Wilson (eds), *Give and Take in Families: studies in resource distribution*, Allen and Unwin, 1987.

60. See note 1.

61. C Vogler, *Labour Market Change and Patterns of Financial Allocation Within Households*, Working Paper no 12, Oxford: ESRC/Social Change and Economic Life Initiative, 1989, quoted in C Glendinning and J Millar (eds), *see* note 1.

62. J Pahl, *Money and Marriage*, Macmillan, 1989.

63. B Campbell, *Wigan Pier Revisited*, Virago, 1984.

64. See note 50.

65. See note 23.

66. See note 62.

67. See note 62.

68. See note 50.

69. S Payne, quoted in R Lister, *see* note 18.

70. *See* R Lister (note 18) for greater detail.

71. A Garnham and E Knights, *Putting the Treasury First, the truth about Child Support*, CPAG Ltd, 1994.

72. The childcare allowance is available to those claiming family credit, disability working allowance, housing benefit and council tax benefit. It is not available to those on income support. See *National Welfare Benefits Handbook 1995/96*, CPAG Ltd, 1995 for details.

73. See note 18.

6 Race and poverty

Despite the high levels of poverty faced by many Black people and members of other minority ethnic groups, there is still relatively little social policy research about race and poverty. *Households below Average Income* – the source of official data about low-income families – contains no breakdown of statistics by ethnic origin.[1] Neither do the *Low Income Statistics*.[2] However, the Department of Social Security's *Family Resources Survey* provides official data which looks at income, social security benefits and ethnic origin.[3] Other important sources of information on racial inequality are the *Labour Force Survey by Ethnic Origin*, the Policy Studies Institute survey 1991/92, the 1991 Census and many useful local surveys.[4]

Below we look at some of the indicators and causes of poverty broken down by ethnic origin. We draw heavily on a report produced by CPAG and the Runnymede Trust called *Poverty in Black and White: deprivation and ethnic minorities*.[5] Throughout this chapter we use the term Black and other minority ethnic groups. However, in text relating to the tables and figures, the terminology used in the source material is retained.

INDICATORS OF POVERTY

UNEMPLOYMENT

Unemployment rates for Black and other minority ethnic groups have been roughly twice that of white people since 1984. The gap has widened slightly since 1993. In 1994, the male unemployment rate for Black people and other minority ethnic groups was 25 per cent, over double the rate for white men, which stood at 11 per cent. The disparity in unemployment rates for women was similar: 16 per cent compared to 7 per cent (see Table 6.1).[6]

TABLE 6.1: **Unemployment rates[1] by sex, age and ethnic origin: average: spring 1994, Great Britain (%)**

	Men		Women	
	All aged 16 and over	16 to 24	All aged 16 and over	16 to 24
White	11	18	7	12
Ethnic minority groups:				
All	25	37	16	27
Black	33	51	18	41
Indian	16	30	12	*
Pakistani/Bangladeshi	29	34	24	*
Mixed – other origins	22	*	16	*

Note: 1. ILO unemployment rates

People who describe thgemselves as Black Caribbean, Black African and Black other (which includes Black British) are grouped together.

*Sample too small

Source: Department of Employment, *Employment Gazette*, 'Ethnic groups and the labour market: analyses from the Spring 1994 Labour Force Survey', DE, June 1995.

- Unemployment rates were highest for Black men (33 per cent), Pakistani/Bangladeshi men (29 per cent) and Pakistani/Bangladeshi women (24 per cent).
- For young people, the unemployment rates are even greater. In 1994, 37 per cent of young men aged between 16 and 24 from Black and other minority ethnic groups were unemployed, compared to 18 per cent of white men. For young women the figures were 27 per cent and 12 per cent respectively. Young Black men and women had extremely high rates of unemployment – one in two young Black men was unemployed (51 per cent) and two out of five young Black women were unemployed (41 per cent).[7]
- Long-term unemployment was also higher among the Black and minority ethnic population – 54 per cent compared to 44 per cent for the white population. The highest rate was among Black people where six out of 10 of the unemployed were long-term unemployed.[8]
- Even with qualifications, Black people and members of other

minority ethnic groups are still more likely to experience unemployment because of discrimination. In 1993, the unemployment rate was 10 per cent for all minority ethnic groups with higher qualifications, and 4 per cent for white people with the same qualifications. For all minority ethnic groups with 'other qualifications', the unemployment rate was 15 per cent compared to 8 per cent for white people who were similarly qualified.[9]

> If you can't be looked at and be seen as white, then you're going to be disadvantaged in employment. It's as simple and easy as that.
>
> (Winston, young black unemployed adult)[10]

LOW PAY AND POOR WORKING CONDITIONS

> I work 40 hours a week in the factory and my take-home pay is between £55 and £66 per week. Last year I started a homeworking job which I can do most evenings and weekends. For this I get paid £15–£20 per week depending on the number of overalls I manage to complete. This money adds towards the household budget and occasionally for clothes for the children ... With the domestic duties and two jobs I have very little time to relax. I don't even have time to fall ill or complain about a backache. I know the work has to be done, as the man would soon come to collect the overalls. My only social life is going to local weddings.
>
> (Mrs P, 42 years old, Asian, with three children)[11]

A sizeable proportion of people living in poverty work in low-paid jobs. On the whole, Black people and other minority ethic groups are more likely to work for low wages than their white counterparts.

The *Labour Force Survey* now contains a question on earnings. Table 6.2, drawn from the *Employment Gazette*, shows the pattern of average full-time hourly earnings by ethnic origin.[12] In 1994, the average hourly pay of all minority ethnic employees was 92 per cent of that of white employees. The differences vary according to the particular ethnic group and gender:

- Pakistani/Bangladeshi employees were lowest paid. Pakistani/Bangladeshi men's earnings were 68 per cent of white men's (£5.47 per hour compared to £8.00 for white men). Pakistani/Bangladeshi women's earnings were 81 per cent of white women's (£5.15 per hour compared to £6.40).
- Black men's earnings were 88 per cent of white men's (£7.03

compared to £8.00 for white men). ('Black' here refers to people of West Indian/Guyanese origin.) However, Black women's earnings were more than white women's – 106 per cent (£6.77 per hour compared to £6.40). Part of the explanation of Black women's higher earnings is that they are more likely to undertake shift work, work longer hours and be based in large unionised public sector workplaces, particularly in London, where wages are often higher. Other research by Irene Bruegel suggests that if numbers of hours and regional differences are taken into account, Black women earn 23 per cent less than white women.[13] Moreover, the available statistics underestimate the extent of low wages among Black women because they do not include homeworking or working in family businesses.[14]

• People of mixed/other origins had earnings that were higher than the white population.[15]

This evidence confirms earlier surveys by the Policy Studies Institute and Leicester City Council that Black and minority ethnic employees were more likely to be low paid (with the exception of Black women).[16] The complex patterns of earnings are affected by a number of factors, in particular the type of occupation and level within that occupation.

TABLE 6.2: **Average earnings of full-time employees by ethnic groups and sex; Great Britain, average of winter 1993/94 to autumn 1994 (not seasonally adjusted)**

£

Ethnic origin	All	Men	Women
Average hourly pay			
All origins	7.42	7.97	6.39
White	7.44	8.00	6.40
Ethnic minority groups	6.82	7.15	6.31
Black	6.92	7.03	6.77
Indian	6.70	7.29	5.77
Pakistani/Bangladeshi	5.39	5.47	5.15
Mixed/other origins	7.70	8.45	6.77
Average hourly pay of ethnic minority groups as			
a percentage of that of the whole population			%
Ethnic minority groups	92	89	99
Black	93	88	106
Indian	90	91	90
Pakistani/Bangladeshi	72	68	81
Mixed/other origins	103	106	106

Source: F Sly, 'Ethnic groups and the labour market', Employment Gazette, June 1995

As well as suffering low pay, substantial proportions of Black and minority ethnic workers experience poor working conditions. Evidence from the 1991/92 Policy Studies Institute survey shows that 20 per cent of minority ethnic employees worked shifts compared to 15 per cent of white employees. The highest proportion was among Pakistani men, 40 per cent of whom worked shifts compared to 18 per cent of white men. Only African Asians were slightly less likely to work shifts (14 per cent). Among women, 19 per cent of African-Caribbeans worked shifts compared to 11 per cent of white women.[17]

> I've worked nights on the wards for years and it really does put a strain on you, there's no question about it. You get a lot of nurses and auxiliaries who suffer from the stress-related illness – hypertension, heart trouble, kidney problems, high blood pressure – you name it, they all come from those broken sleep patterns from the night shift. You can't just go home and go to sleep during the day if you've got kids. When you come in from work, you've got to get them ready for school, do the shopping, do the housework, do the washing, and by the time you've finished it's three o'clock and time to collect them from school again, so you just don't get any rest... What happens is you just adjust in time to getting less sleep than everyone else, but over the years that takes its toll.
>
> (B Bryan *et al*, *The Heart of the Race*)[18]

BENEFITS

The *Family Resources Survey* provides official information for the first time about benefit claimants and ethnic origin.[19] Dependence on means-tested benefits is one important indicator of low income. Table 6.3 shows that Black and minority ethnic groups are much more likely to be reliant on the key safety-net benefit, income support, reflecting their higher rates of unemployment. Over half of Pakistani/Bangladeshi households received income support (54 per cent), over triple the proportion of white households (17 per cent). High proportions of Black Caribbeans and Black Africans also relied on income support – 39 per cent and 36 per cent respectively. Only Indian households had a slightly lower rate – 25 per cent were receiving income support. The figures for family credit suggest that there are high rates of low pay among Pakistani/Bangladeshi families – 11 per cent of households in this group were receiving family credit, compared to 2 per cent of white households. On the whole, minority ethnic groups were also more reliant on housing benefit – with the exception of Indian households, reflecting higher rates of owner occupation. There is some evidence to suggest that people from minority ethnic groups are less likely to claim benefits to which they are entitled, so these figures are likely to underestimate the extent of their poverty.

The higher rates of child benefit receipt among the ethnic minority population (as high as 77 per cent among the Pakistani/Bangladeshi households compared to 31 per cent of white households), and lower figures for retirement pension, reveal the younger age profile of minority groups.[20]

TABLE 6.3: **Proportion of households receiving benefit by ethnic origin in 1993/94**

%

Household	White	Black Caribbean	Black African	Indian	Pakistani/ Bangladeshi	Other	All
IS	17	39	36	25	54	35	18
FC	2	3	4	4	11	1	2
HB	19	40	46	12	24	27	20
CTB	37	40	38	23	42	37	37
RP	30	14	1	9	4	7	29
CB	31	47	54	62	77	47	32
OPB	4	16	17	5	4	8	5

IS: income support, FC: family credit, HB: housing benefit, CTB: council tax benefit, RP: retirement pension, CB: child benefit, OPB: one parent benefit

Source: Analysis by DSS, *Family Resources Survey, 1993/94*, Table 2.19, HMSO, 1995.

INCOME

The *Family Resources Survey* also provides material about income and ethnic origin.[21] Overall, it broadly suggests that *some* minority ethnic groups are more likely to be on lower incomes than white households. (The data need to be treated with caution as they are based on gross income figures and are not adjusted for family size.) In 1993/94, 52 per cent of Black Caribbeans and 49 per cent of Black Africans had gross incomes of under £200 a week compared to 41 per cent of white households. However, only 21 per cent of Indian households had incomes below this level. It appears that Black Caribbean, Black African and Pakistani households are also less likely to have higher incomes: 16 per cent of Black Caribbeans, 15 per cent of Black Africans and 13 per cent of Pakistani/Bangladeshi households had gross incomes of over £500 a week. Twenty-seven per cent of Indian households had gross incomes above £500 a week. This confirms the picture found in the Rowntree Inquiry into Income and Wealth which also found that some minority ethnic groups were more likely to be concentrated at lower levels of income than the white population.[22]

CAUSES OF POVERTY

The persistence of high levels of poverty for Black people and other minority ethnic groups is due to a number of factors:

- Immigration policy has curtailed access to welfare services, forcing some people to rely on their family for support.
- Inequalities in the labour market are founded on deeply-embedded discriminatory employment practices. This has left Black people highly exposed to the economic restructuring which has taken place through the 1980s and early 1990s.
- Family patterns and the age structure of minority ethnic groups mean that some groups are more likely to be vulnerable to policies which have had a detrimental effect on families with children and on young people.
- Social security policies have been directly and indirectly discriminatory, leaving many Black people without support from the state.
- The racism and discrimination in society as a whole often exclude Black people from employment opportunities and access to welfare.

IMMIGRATION POLICY AND POVERTY

The prevailing ideology was that Black people had come 'individually and on their own initiative' and thus there was no need to make welfare provision for them. There was thus *no intention* to provide for them, and when Black immigrants did use welfare services they were seen as scroungers.

(Fiona Williams: *Social Policy: A Critical Introduction*)[23]

Black people's experience of poverty in the UK has been fundamentally shaped by immigration policy.[24] Immigration policy has attempted
to reduce the 'social costs' of people who come to work in the UK,
either by curbing access to welfare services or by restricting the right
to bring dependants to this country. After the 1971 Immigration Act,
the wives and children of Commonwealth citizens could only enter
the United Kingdom if a sponsor could support and accommodate
them without recourse to 'public funds'. 'Public funds' – clearly
defined for the first time in 1985 – consisted of supplementary benefit
(now income support), housing benefit, family income supplement
(now family credit) and housing under Part III of the Housing Act
1985 (Housing the Homeless). The definition of 'public funds' is now
being extended to include other benefits (see p127). The effect of
these policies has been to cause great financial hardship to those
struggling to survive without help from the state. These policies have
also meant that some families have been forced to live apart in
different parts of the world because UK citizens cannot afford to
support dependants without some support from the state. Alongside
these changes, harsher rules on who is allowed to seek asylum in this
country have been introduced (see p128). More fundamentally, the
legislation has reinforced a climate of opinion where Black people
are seen as 'outsiders', unwelcome in British society.

INEQUALITY IN THE LABOUR MARKET

Immigrant workers were sucked into the economy where they were
needed, whatever their qualifications – into those jobs that white
people were becoming less inclined to do. The availability of jobs
during labour shortages therefore laid the basis for the occupational
inequalities that have persisted since.

(C Brown, *Race Relations and Discrimination*)[25]

The poverty of Black people and minority ethnic groups is rooted in
old inequalities in the labour market. Many still work in the
manufacturing and manual work for which they were recruited in
the 1950s and 1960s. The segregation of some minority ethnic
workers into certain industries and into manual work has exposed
them particularly to both the decline in manufacturing and the rise
in unemployment (unemployment is a much higher risk for people
in manual work). People from minority ethnic groups are also much
more likely to be living in inner-city areas and have therefore borne

the brunt of industry's exodus from city centres. However, patterns of employment have changed markedly in the 1980s and 1990s and the position of minority ethnic groups is becoming more differentiated both *between* and *within* minority groups.[26] Labour market inequalities stem from segregation by industry and by job level. Below we look at both these forms of segregation.

Many of the industries where some minority ethnic groups are concentrated pay very low wages. The 1993 Policy Studies Institute report shows that in 1988–90:[27]

- 22 per cent of minority ethnic men worked in distribution, hotels, catering and repairs compared to 15 per cent of white men. The proportion was much higher among Bangladeshi and Chinese men (53 per cent). The 1994 *New Earnings Survey* shows that 26 per cent of full-time male employees in this industrial sector earned less that £170 a week (the average for all industries is 11 per cent).[28]
- 14 per cent of minority ethnic men worked in other manufacturing compared to 10 per cent of white men. Within this sector 15 per cent of Bangladeshi men worked in clothing and footwear compared to 1 per cent of white men. Twenty-seven per cent of male employees in this industrial sector earned less than £170 a week.[29]
- 22 per cent of minority ethnic women worked in distribution, hotels, catering and repairs compared to 25 per cent of white women. However, certain groups, such as Pakistani and Chinese women, were much more likely to work in this area – 33 per cent and 41 per cent respectively. Thirty-five per cent of female employees in this industrial sector earned less than £130 a week (the average for all industries is 22 per cent of the female manual workforce earning less than £130 a week).[30]
- 22 per cent of Pakistani women worked in clothing and footwear compared to 2 per cent of white women. Thirty-three per cent of employees in this industrial sector earned less than £130 a week.[31]

Research by Reena Bhavnani on labour market prospects suggests that Black women will not benefit from the expected rise in part-time jobs for women:

> Black women are to be found in occupations which are in decline, and are under-represented in the growth areas ... The abolition of Wages Councils, the growth of competitive tendering and the

restructuring of finance and other white-collar work indicates that black women may increase their employment levels but in a deteriorating situation.[32]

The Policy Studies Institute report shows that while minority ethnic groups as a whole have *lower* job levels than the white population, there are some exceptions to this pattern.[33] In 1988–90:

- 21 per cent of minority ethnic men fall into the category of professional/manager/employer compared to 27 per cent of white men. Only 12 per cent of African-Caribbean and Pakistani and Bangladeshi men are at this job level. However, men from some groups have broadly the same or higher proportions at these occupational levels: Chinese (30 per cent), other mixed (30 per cent), African Asian (27 per cent) and Indian (25 per cent). Among women, 9 per cent of minority ethnic women fall into the professional/manager/employer category compared to 11 per cent of white women, while 16 per cent of Chinese women and 12 per cent of other mixed fell into this group.
- 23 per cent of minority ethnic men fall into the category of semi-skilled manual compared to 15 per cent of white men. The difference is much more marked among some groups – 65 per cent of Bangladeshi men and 36 per cent of Chinese men fall into this category. Twenty-seven per cent of minority ethnic women are semi-skilled compared to 22 per cent of white women. Again there are much higher percentages among certain groups: 45 per cent of Pakistani women, 34 per cent of Indian women and 32 per cent of African women.

While some minority ethnic groups have entered higher job levels, for people of African-Caribbean, Pakistani and Bangladeshi origin inequality in the labour market remains firmly entrenched.

FAMILY PATTERNS

The age profile of Black people is younger than that of white people. In 1991:[34]

- 22 per cent of Black Caribbean, 29 per cent of Black African, 51 per cent of Black other, 30 per cent of Indian, 43 per cent of Pakistani, 47 per cent of Bangladeshi and 19 per cent of white people were aged under 15;
- 28 per cent of Black Caribbean, 32 per cent of Black African, 31

per cent of Black other, 24 per cent of Indian, 24 per cent of Pakistani, 24 per cent of Bangladeshi and 20 per cent of white people were aged between 16 and 29;

- 11 per cent of Black Caribbean, 3 per cent of Black African, 2 per cent of Black other, 7 per cent of Indian, 4 per cent of Pakistani, 3 per cent of Bangladeshi and 22 per cent of white people were aged 60 and above.

The younger age profile means that Black people and people from other minority ethnic groups are disproportionately affected by government policies such as past freezes in child benefit and cuts in income support for young people. On the other hand, there are fewer Black and other minority ethnic people among pensioners. However, although fewer in number, Black pensioners are more likely than white pensioners to be living on lower incomes because of social security rules which are indirectly discriminatory. As the Black and minority ethnic population grows older, more will become vulnerable to the poverty which afflicts pensioners.

Family patterns also vary considerably between different ethnic groups. For example, lone parenthood is lower among Asian people than white people, but higher among people of West Indian and African origin (8 per cent of Bangladeshi and Pakistani families; 6 per cent of Indian; 49 per cent of West Indian; 30 per cent of African; 18 per cent of all ethnic minority families; and 15 per cent of white families).[35]

As we have seen, the risks of poverty are much higher among lone mothers than other groups. Women's lower wages, coupled with few and expensive childcare facilities, force many lone parents to stay on benefit. So the risks of poverty which accompany lone parenthood are particularly acute for Black women.

The Policy Studies Institute survey found that in 1988–90 the average number of children in minority ethnic households was higher than in white households:

- 14 per cent of minority ethnic households had three or more dependent children compared to 4 per cent of white households.
- 35 per cent of Pakistani and Bangladeshi households had three or more dependent children.[36]

As we have seen, the rise in child poverty over the last decade was steeper than the rise among the whole population. Over the same period, data also show very sharp rises in poverty among children in families composed of couples with three or more children. Yet again, because a greater proportion of minority ethnic households comprise families with children they have been disproportionately exposed to the rise in child poverty.

DISCRIMINATION IN SOCIAL SECURITY

A couple who originally came from Pakistan but now have British nationality were deprived of benefit when the man returned from Pakistan after a long visit to see family. The couple had six children yet were left with only their child benefit as income. The man had a history of 23 years' employment in the UK. The decision to refuse benefit was eventually reversed but not before the family had suffered considerable hardship.[37]

The social security system discriminates both directly and indirectly against Black people, in many cases leaving people from minority ethnic groups exposed to economic and social hardships without the protection of benefits. Today's social security system, still shaped by Beveridge's vision of a homogeneous society of white, UK-born, full-time male workers, is ill-equipped to deal with society's various needs in the 1990s.

CONTRIBUTORY BENEFITS

Much of our social security system is founded on the contributory principle, whereby people receive national insurance benefits such as unemployment benefit and retirement pension in return for contributions made from earnings. In practice, a contributory scheme tends to discriminate against people who are in intermittent and/or low-paid work. Currently, anyone who earns below the national insurance threshold of £58 a week in 1995/96 does not make any contributions, and therefore does not receive any contributory benefits. In addition, because contributions are earnings-related, people in lower-paid jobs take longer to satisfy the contribution conditions than people in higher-paid jobs. As we have seen, people from minority ethnic groups are more likely to be in low-paid work and face a much higher risk of unemployment. The result is that they often have less access to contributory benefits. For example, many Black and other minority ethnic group pensioners are forced to rely on means-tested support in retirement. Figures from an earlier

Policy Studies Institute survey show that fewer Asians and West Indians than white people claimed retirement pension and that, as a result, a quarter of Asians and West Indians of pensionable age were dependent on supplementary pension.[38]

In addition, for many people from minority ethnic groups, sustaining family links involves paying visits abroad. Such visits, however, have important consequences for entitlement to contributory benefits as they often mean breaks in contributions. Thus, many people from minority ethnic groups are excluded from contributory benefits which have important advantages over other types of benefits – in that they are not means-tested and are paid on an individual basis.

NON-CONTRIBUTORY BENEFITS

These benefits have residence and/or presence conditions attached to them. These tests were once very tough indeed. For example, until recently, to claim severe disablement allowance a claimant had to prove residence in the UK for 10 out of the preceding 20 years. However, in 1992 the rules were changed and now a person must be 'ordinarily resident' and have been present in Britain for a continuous period of six months before claiming.

Other non-contributory benefits such as child benefit were specifically aimed at people present in the UK. (Previously child tax allowances were payable for children supported outside the United Kingdom.) Often people living in this country are still supporting family members in their countries of origin. Since such obligations are not recognised by our social security system, this can mean struggling to survive on much reduced incomes.

MEANS-TESTED BENEFITS

The 'public funds' and sponsorship rules illustrate the close links between access to benefits and immigration. Under our immigration rules, most people admitted to the UK can enter on condition that they do not rely on 'public funds',[39] which include the main means-tested benefits. If receipt of these benefits becomes known to the Home Office it may affect the person's right to stay, to get an extension of leave or a change in conditions of stay, or result in leave being curtailed. The public funds test is now incorporated into income support, housing benefit and council tax benefit.

Certain groups of people coming to the UK have to be sponsored by a relative or friend. The introduction of 'sponsors' had a crucial impact on minority ethnic groups' access and entitlement to welfare support. It is, in fact, only in a minority of cases that such sponsorship is legally binding, although many people mistakenly believe it to be so. If a sponsor is legally liable but fails to maintain the sponsee, the Benefits Agency has the power to recover income support paid to the sponsee. However, if the sponsor cannot afford to pay then the Benefits Agency should not pursue the matter. The immigration legislation which introduced the concept of a sponsor has meant that many minority ethnic families have been and are divided across continents. There is now a considerable body of evidence documenting the contact between the DSS and the Home Office. Passport checks on Black claimants – whether or not they were born in the UK – have become a frequent occurrence at Benefits Agency offices.

Recent proposals exclude some sponsored immigrants and asylum-seekers from entitlement to income support, housing benefit and council tax benefit.[40] Access to non-contributory benefits – attendance allowance, disability working allowance, disability living allowance, invalid care allowance and severe disablement allowance – is also to be restricted to certain groups, largely British, Irish, European Union and European Economic Area nationals, refugees and people with exceptional leave to remain. The government is introducing primary legislation to restrict access to child benefit again, mainly to the same groups listed above. The rules for sponsorship will be similar; anyone who enters the UK subject to sponsorship will be excluded from all means-tested and non-contributory benefits.[41]

Alongside these measures the government proposes to curtail the rights of asylum-seekers to benefit. All those who seek asylum after entering the UK (some 70 per cent of all asylum-seekers) will no longer be entitled to any benefits. This measure will affect around 28,000 refugees and their dependants. In addition, if asylum applicants receive a negative decision from the Home Office, they too will no longer be able to claim benefit.[42]

These changes follow on from the introduction of the habitual residence test in 1994 as a condition of entitlement for income-related benefits for most claimants. The criteria for satisfying the test include: the person's centre of interest, their employment history and nature of employment in the UK and their length and continuity of residence elsewhere. Some minority ethnic groups are more likely to make visits abroad as their families are spread across different continents. Aimed at so-called 'benefit tourism', the test has had a particularly detrimental effect on Black and minority ethnic groups.[43]

THE 1988 SOCIAL SECURITY CHANGES

The overhaul of social security in 1988 accentuated the emphasis on means-testing and has meant greater hardship for many Black and other minority ethnic claimants:

- Under income support the removal of most 16- and 17-year-olds' right to benefit except in cases of severe hardship and the lower rate of benefit for under 25s are indirectly discriminatory because Black and other minority ethnic groups have a higher proportion of people who fall into this age-group.
- The social fund brought in discretion and no independent right of appeal and hence greater scope for racism.[44]
- Questions on the date of arrival in this country have been added to the income support form.
- People from minority ethnic groups may well be underclaiming family credit because it relies on claimants providing a great deal of evidence about their employment. Many people from minority ethnic groups work in low-paying sectors of the economy; some of their employers may not pay tax and national insurance and thus may be reluctant to provide information for employees.
- The state earnings-related pension scheme (SERPS) has been weakened and is based on a lifetime's earnings instead of the 'best 20 years' rule. This indirectly discriminates against minority ethnic groups. People who have come to this country in their thirties and forties will have a shorter working life and thus a lower retirement pension.
- The inducements to take up private pensions merely reinforce existing inequalities in the labour market and thus do not benefit the majority of people from minority ethnic groups.

These are only some of the difficulties that are caused by the benefits system. In addition, the extension of means-testing exacerbates all the problems associated with the link between immigration status and entitlement to benefit. The further social security intrudes into the minutiae of individual circumstances the more room there is for racism. Some Black people, excluded from all help under the new system, find themselves placed firmly in the category of the 'undeserving poor'.

ADMINISTRATION OF SOCIAL SECURITY

The administration of social security often discriminates directly or indirectly against people from minority ethnic groups.

> There is no doubt that they don't look well on us people and that is why it takes so long to get an answer from them, or when it's late they take even longer. It's more difficult if you don't know the language or can't read or write English.
>
> (R Cohen *et al, Hardship Britain: being poor in the 1990s*)[45]

A report by the National Association of Citizens Advice Bureaux (NACAB) identified a number of key difficulties with how social security is administered: communication, delays in benefit payments, late claims, wrongful refusal of benefit and underclaiming of benefits.[46]

The NACAB survey identified low take-up as an important problem for people from minority ethnic groups. There is growing evidence of low take-up.[47] Fear of creating problems, concern that any fuss might affect the chance to stay and the lack of translated material have created a climate in which people from minority ethnic groups are less likely to assert their rights, often doubting their entitlement to benefits.

The National Audit Office commissioned National Opinion Polls to undertake a survey of family credit recipients (a means-tested benefit which goes to people in paid work, which replaced family income supplement in 1988). It found that only 69 per cent of minority ethnic claimants received help with free prescriptions and only 44 per cent received help with free dental care, compared to 74 per cent and 62 per cent of white claimants respectively.[48]

In 1989/90, the Family Service Units interviewed 32 Asian families living on income support in Bradford.[49] They found that 26 of them had made no application to the social fund (the social fund provides some community care grants, but mainly loans, for people on income support). Azra Sadiq-Sangster writes:

> Most of the Asians did not want to take on social fund loans, especially as payments would be deducted from their benefits. Many were not aware of the social fund but, when told about it, they said they would not consider taking it up because they feared having less money on a weekly basis for the sake of a lump sum.[50]

DISCRIMINATION AND RACISM

Racial discrimination remains widespread and 'pernicious' to use the Prime Minister's term, and so far from being redundant the Race Relations Act as at present formulated does not provide a strong enough basis for dealing with it.

(Sir Michael Day OBE, Commission for Racial Equality)[51]

The legal framework for dealing with racism – beginning with the 1965 and 1968 Race Relations Acts and strengthened by the 1976 Act – has had little impact on the levels of discrimination in employment.

Research carried out by the Commission for Racial Equality and Policy Studies Institute suggests that discrimination was not fundamentally reduced in the 1980s. In 1984/85, the PSI looked at 100 employers offering a wide range of manual and non-manual jobs in London, Birmingham and Manchester and found that a white applicant was over a third more likely to receive a positive response than an ethnic minority applicant. The research found that at least a third of employers discriminated against Asian and African-Caribbean applicants.[52] The levels of discrimination found in this study were similar to those found in research carried out in the 1970s. This research only measured direct discrimination. It gives no indication of the level of indirect discrimination which may affect people from minority ethnic groups. Thus, despite legislation, the prevalence of discrimination had not declined. Colin Brown explains:

We are constantly driven back to the ugly fact of direct racial discrimination, which persists and acts on people's lives whenever it has the chance. It may be that the more subtle aspects of racial inequality have been stressed too much, or too soon. While the main problem of British race relations is, plainly and simply, discrimination based on racial hostility.[53]

British Social Attitudes attempts to document the extent of racism today. It reveals a strong feeling that racism is widespread, but that it is in decline. It found that in 1991:

- around half of the people surveyed thought there was a lot of prejudice against African-Caribbeans and slightly more against Asians;
- there had been a sharp decline in the proportion of respondents thinking that prejudice was more widespread than five years before;

- there was a small decrease in reported prejudice; however, a third of the sample still admitted to being either 'very prejudiced' or 'a little prejudiced' against people of other races;
- there was an increase in the support for anti-discrimination law with 76 per cent supporting it.[54]

CONCLUSION

Every indicator of poverty shows that Black people and people from other minority ethnic groups are more at risk of unemployment, low pay, poor conditions at work and diminished social security rights. Their poverty is caused by discriminatory immigration policies which have often excluded people from abroad from access to welfare; employment patterns which have marginalised Black people and other minority ethnic groups into low-paid manual work; direct and indirect discrimination in social security; and the broader experience of racism in society as a whole.

Tackling poverty among Black and other minority ethnic groups is about both general policies for reducing poverty – such as reducing unemployment or introducing a minimum wage – and about specific policies. CPAG believes the following specific policies would begin to reduce racial inequality:

- New employment opportunities and training programmes aimed at Black and other minority ethnic groups.
- The strengthening of anti-discrimination laws in line with the Commission for Racial Equality's recommendations which include: extending legal aid to industrial tribunals; providing clearer definitions of indirect discrimination; the introduction of contract compliance as in the Fair Employment legislation in Northern Ireland; and extending the scope of the 1976 Race Relations Act to cover all areas of government activity.
- The abolition of discriminatory aspects of the social security system.
- The translation of a wide variety of leaflets into minority languages, an obligation on the part of the Benefits Agency to provide interpreters, increasing advice work at community centres and take-up campaigns that specifically cater for the complex and diverse needs of the Black and other minority ethnic communities.[55]
- A draft directive in Europe which forbids discrimination in social

security (both in social assistance and insurance-based schemes) against people from minority ethnic groups.

- The European Community Charter of Fundamental Human Rights should contain a commitment to ending racial inequality.

NOTES

1. *Households below Average Income, a statistical analysis, 1979–1992/93*, Government Statistical Service, HMSO, 1995, and revised edition, 1995.
2. Social Security Committee, First Report, *Low Income Statistics: Low Income Families 1989–1992*, HMSO, 1995.
3. DSS, *Family Resources Survey, Great Britain 1993/94*, HMSO, 1995.
4. *Labour Force Surveys*, Department for Education and Employment, published annually with a summary in the *Employment Gazette*; and T Jones, *Britain's Ethnic Minorities*, Policy Studies Institute, 1993.
5. K Amin with C Oppenheim, *Poverty in Black and White, deprivation and ethnic minorities*, CPAG Ltd in association with the Runnymede Trust, 1992.
6. F Sly, 'Ethnic groups and the labour market: analyses from the 1994 Labour Force Survey', *Employment Gazette, June 1995*, Department of Employment, HMSO, 1995.
7. *See* note 6.
8. *See* note 6.
9. F Sly, 'Ethnic groups and the labour market', *Employment Gazette, May 1994*, Department of Employment, HMSO, 1995.
10. S McRae, *Young and Jobless*, Policy Studies Institute, 1987.
11. *Last among equals*, West Midlands Low Pay Unit, 1988.
12. *See* note 6.
13. I Bruegel, 'Sex and race in the labour market', *Feminist Review*, No 32, Summer 1989.
14. R Bhavnani, *Black Women in the Labour Market: a research review*, Equal Opportunities Commission, 1994.
15. *See* note 6.
16. K B Duffy, I C Lincoln, *Earnings and Ethnicity*, Principal Report on Research Commissioned by Leicester City Council, 1990.
17. *See* note 4.
18. B Bryan, S Dadzie, S Scafe, *The Heart of the Race*, Virago, 1985.
19. *See* note 2.
20. *See* note 2.
21. *See* note 2.
22. J Hills, *Inquiry into Income and Wealth Vol 2*, Joseph Rowntree Foundation, 1995.
23. F Williams, *Social Policy: a critical introduction*, Polity Press, 1989,

quoted in N Ginsburg, *Divisions of Welfare: a critical introduction to comparative social policy*, Sage Publications Ltd, 1992.

24. For details on immigration policy, *see* P Gordon and F Klug, *British Immigration Control: a brief guide*, Runnymede Trust, 1985.

25. C Brown, 'Race relations and discrimination' in *Policy Studies*, Vol 11, No 2, Policy Studies Institute, Summer 1990.

26. *See* note 4.

27. *See* note 4.

28. Department of Employment, *New Earnings Survey 1994 Parts C and D*, HMSO, 1995.

29. *See* note 28.

30. *See* note 28.

31. *See* note 28.

32. *See* note 14.

33. *See* note 4.

34. *Social Trends 1994*, HMSO, 1994.

35. J Haskey, 'Estimated numbers and demographic characteristics of one-parent families in Great Britain', *Population Trends No 65*, Autumn 1991, HMSO, 1991.

36. *See* note 4.

37. B Lakhani, *CPAG Briefing: Habitual Residence Regulations*, CPAG, 1994.

38. C Brown, *Black and White Britain, the third PSI Survey*, Policy Studies Institute, Gower, 1984.

39. *National Welfare Benefits Handbook 1995/96*, CPAG Ltd, 1995.

40. The Social Security (Persons from Abroad) Miscellaneous Amendments Regulations, 1996.

41. DSS, *Explanatory memorandum to the Social Security Advisory Committee, Social Security (Persons from Abroad) Miscellaneous Amendment Regulations, 1995*.

42. See note 41.

43. *See* note 37.

44. S Conlan, 'Without recourse to public funds: immigration and social security since the Second World War', unpublished dissertation, Leicester University, 1989.

45. R Cohen, J Coxall, G Craig and A Sadiq-Sangster, *Hardship Britain: being poor in the 1990s*, CPAG Ltd in association with FSU, 1992.

46. NACAB, *Barriers to Benefit: black claimants and social security*, NACAB, 1991.

47. I Law *et al*, *Racial Equality and Social Security Delivery: a study of the perceptions and experiences of black minority ethnic people eligible for benefit in Leeds*, Sociology and Social Policy Research Working Paper 10, University of Leeds, 1994.

48. National Opinion Polls, 'A survey of family credit recipients for the

National Audit Office', *Support for Low Income Families*, HMSO, 1991.

49. *See* note 45.
50. A Sadiq-Sangster, *Surviving on Income Support, the Asian experience*, Family Service Units, 1991.
51. Commission for Racial Equality, *The Second Review of the Race Relations Act 1976*, CRE, 1992.
52. C Brown and P Gray, *Racial Discrimination: 17 years after the Act*, Policy Studies Institute, 1985.
53. *See* note 25.
54. *See* note 25.
55. K Young, 'Class, race and opportunity' in R Jowell *et al* (eds), *British Social Attitudes, the 9th report*, 1992/93 edn, SCPR, Dartmouth, 1992.

7 The geography of poverty

... it must never be forgotten that the roots of poverty are not straightforwardly to be found within the places and regions affected ... Rather, the causes of poverty 'in place' derive from many different sources and locations beyond that place, and this must be taken on board in policy formulation and execution.

(C Philo et al, '"Poor places" and beyond')[1]

The scale and nature of poverty depend partly on where you live. Living standards are not evenly spread across the country, or within each city, town or village. Even in areas of affluence, pockets of poverty are evident. Identifying a geography of poverty is not a straightforward task.[2]

Regional disparities have become more distinct as a result of the rapid changes in our economic structure, in particular the decline of industrial manufacturing. A North–South divide persists[3] but it has been moderated slightly by the disproportionate impact of the early 1990s recession on the South East.

In addition, there are, of course, large differences *within* regions. This is particularly evident in the South East where there is a juxtaposition of extreme poverty and wealth (compare the living standards of those living in different London boroughs, for example). At an even more localised level, living standards can vary to an even greater extent. Anne Green's work[4] found increasing polarisation of living standards between wards (neighbourhoods with an average population of around 5,000) during the 1980s.

THE REGIONAL ECONOMY

Despite the impact of the most recent recession, the South East remains dominant in our national economy. The chart below illustrates the gross domestic product (GDP) per head for each region compared to the figure for the whole of the UK in 1993.[5] The South East had the highest level of GDP per head, while Northern Ireland had the lowest.

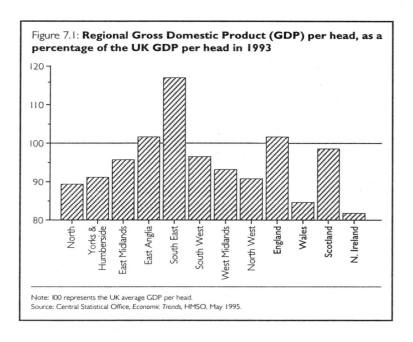

Figure 7.1: **Regional Gross Domestic Product (GDP) per head, as a percentage of the UK GDP per head in 1993**

Note: 100 represents the UK average GDP per head.
Source: Central Statistical Office, *Economic Trends*, HMSO, May 1995.

There are no comprehensive up-to-date poverty statistics broken down by region. The government has not provided an analysis of *Households below Average Income* (see Chapter 2) by region. Instead, we look at a number of deprivation indicators: the number of children receiving free school meals, average incomes and unemployment rates.

FREE SCHOOL MEALS

One indication of child poverty in the regions is the number and proportion of children receiving a free school meal. Children in families living on income support are entitled to free school meals. Table 7.1 below shows which regions have the highest proportion of primary school children getting free meals.[6] Northern Ireland had the highest rates, with just under one in three primary school children receiving free school meals. Wales and the North followed with 25 per cent and 24 per cent respectively. The regions with the lowest proportions of primary school children eating free school meals were: West Midlands (14 per cent), East Anglia (14 per cent) and the South West (15 per cent).

TABLE 7.1: **The number and proportion of children on the school roll receiving free school meals in 1994 in primary schools***

	Numbers	%
North	69,965	24
Yorkshire & Humberside	89,220	19
North West	148,296	23
East Midlands	54,456	15
West Midlands	71,399	14
East Anglia	24,031	14
South East	301,813	20
South West	56,249	15
England	815,436	19
Wales	72,246	25
Scotland	456,890	23
Northern Ireland	57,894	30

Note: 'primary' includes nursery schools and middle schools.
*Source: Data provided by Department for Education and Employment and from Welsh, Scottish and Northern Ireland Offices.

Yet again, these figures underestimate the extent of childhood deprivation because of non-take up of benefits. Some families with children do not take up their entitlement to income support and some families with children who *are* receiving income support do not take up their entitlement to free school meals. In 1993, the take-up of free school meals by those authorised to do so was as low as 6 per cent in some boroughs.[7]

There are, of course, important differences within regions. Urban areas have higher rates of children on free meals than non-urban areas. For example, 43 per cent of children in primary schools in Manchester were receiving free school meals, compared to 9 per cent in Dorset.[8]

INCOME

The *Family Expenditure Survey* for 1994–95 contains useful data for the regions.[9] Table 7.2 shows the average proportion of household income derived from social security benefits in each region. Whereas on average a fifth of average household income comes from social security for households in Wales, in the South East the percentage of household income derived from benefits is much smaller – a tenth.

TABLE 7.2: **Social security benefits income as a percentage of gross weekly household income 1994-95**

	%
North	19.2
Yorkshire & Humberside	15.5
East Midlands	12.1
East Anglia	12.8
South East	10.1
South West	11.6
West Midlands	15.9
North West	15.7
Wales	22.5
Scotland	15.2
Northern Ireland	19.6
United Kingdom	13.5

Source: Central Statistical Office, *Family Spending. A report on the 1994-95 Family Expenditure Survey*, Government Statistical Service, HMSO, 1995.

These regional patterns are borne out by the average household income in each region and how it compares to the average for the UK (see Table 7.3).[10] Household income in Wales is about three-quarters of the average for the UK. Incomes in the North and the West Midlands are also well below the UK average. Meanwhile, household income in the South East is 18 per cent higher than the UK average.

TABLE 7.3: **Average gross normal weekly household income by region in 1994-95**

	£ per week	as a % of UK income
North	303.95	82
Yorkshire & Humberside	343.35	93
East Midlands	365.84	99
East Anglia	345.58	94
South East	435.41	118
South West	378.85	102
West Midlands	321.85	87
North West	340.85	92
Wales	282.74	76
Scotland	362.96	98
Northern Ireland	354.12	96
UK	369.25	100

Source: Central Statistical Office, *Family Spending, A report on the 1994/95 Family Expenditure Survey*, Government Statistical Service, HMSO, 1995.

Research undertaken for the Rowntree Inquiry into Income and Wealth[11] has shown that when regional price differences and housing costs are taken into account the differences between regions is reduced by about 70 per cent.

Alissa Goodman and Steven Webb at the Institute for Fiscal Studies have looked at changes in regional incomes over time using data from the *Family Expenditure Survey*.[12] Over the period 1961–1991 they found an improvement in relative incomes for those living in the South (South East, South West, East Anglia), particularly between the end of the 1970s and mid-1980s. By the early 1990s mean incomes in Southern England were around one quarter higher than those in the Midlands and the North. Scottish incomes markedly improved in the mid 1970s but were broadly stable thereafter. Incomes in the Midlands fell from above to below average. However, about a third of the widening gap between regions over this period can be explained by the regional differences in inflation rates.[13]

EMPLOYMENT AND UNEMPLOYMENT

The structure of employment has changed radically in recent years with a major shift away from traditional manufacturing industry.

This explains the persistence of higher rates of unemployment in regions and countries which were centres of manufacturing industry.[14]

- In the United Kingdom, manufacturing accounted for 20 per cent of all employment in 1992, down from 32 per cent in 1976.
- The Midlands and the North, North West, Yorkshire and Humberside had the highest concentration of employment in manufacturing in 1976 (between a third and nearly half of those in employment were in manufacturing).
- Service industries have increased from 57 to 73 per cent of total employment over the same period. The rise of the new industries has been much more pronounced in the South East and South West than in the traditional manufacturing strongholds.

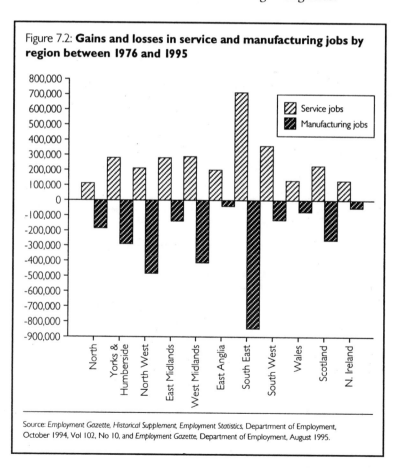

Figure 7.2: **Gains and losses in service and manufacturing jobs by region between 1976 and 1995**

Source: *Employment Gazette, Historical Supplement, Employment Statistics*, Department of Employment, October 1994, Vol 102, No 10, and *Employment Gazette*, Department of Employment, August 1995.

Overall, dividing the country into the 'North' and 'South', the 'North' lost 64 per cent of all the manufacturing jobs that have disappeared between 1976 and 1995 (1,763,000 jobs) while the South lost 36 per cent (996,000). The South gained 53 per cent of all the new service jobs that were gained since 1976 (1,551,000) while the North gained 47 per cent (1,385,000). Figure 7.2 illustrates the gains and losses in manufacturing and service jobs for each region between 1976 and 1995.

TABLE 7.4: **Unemployment rates in 1966, 1976, 1986 and 1995, by region**

	1966	1976	1986	1995
North	2.4	5.3	15.4	10.6
Yorkshire & Humberside	1.1	3.9	12.6	8.9
North West	1.4	5.1	13.8	8.8
East Midlands	1.0	3.5	9.9	7.6
West Midlands	0.8	4.3	12.6	8.4
East Anglia	1.4	3.5	8.1	6.4
South East	0.9	3.1	8.3	8.0
South West	1.7	4.7	9.5	7.3
England	N/A	3.9	11.3	8.2
Wales	2.7	5.3	13.9	8.3
Scotland	2.7	5.1	13.4	8.1
Northern Ireland	N/A	7.1	17.4	11.8
United Kingdom	N/A	4.2	11.2	8.3

Note: 1995 figures are seasonally adjusted for April 1995; the other dates are based on an annual average
Source: Central Statistical Office, *Regional Trends*, Table 10.19, HMSO, 1990 edition, and *Employment Gazette*, Department of Employment, July 1995

In other words, those areas that have been most impoverished by the dismantling of manufacturing industries have also gained least from the development of new forms of employment.

Not surprisingly, regional and national inequalities are reflected in patterns of unemployment. In April 1995, Northern Ireland had the worst unemployment rate at 11.8 per cent, and was followed by the North with 10.6 per cent (see Table 7.4).[15] The pattern of unemployment between the regions has changed. The recession of the early 1980s which brought unemployment to its highest levels in 1986 increased the disparity between the regions. The dramatic fall in manufacturing employment hit the 'North' most severely. Un-employment had fallen in all regions in the mid-1980s but had fallen more rapidly in the North than the South. *The recession of the early 1990s has hit the South East with a heavier blow; the result is a narrowing of the unemployment rates between regions.* For example, in 1986 the gap between the lowest rate of unemployment in East Anglia and the highest in the North (we are leaving out Northern Ireland as it has had persistently high unemployment) was 7.3 per cent; today that gap is 5.4 per cent. The unemployment rate in the South East is just below the average for the UK. Figure 7.3 shows the merging of unemployment rates which has marked this recession.

Rates of redundancies in the different regions also illustrate the changing regional pattern. In spring 1994, the highest redundancy rate was in the Northern region. While redundancy rates have fallen throughout all regions, they have fallen faster in Greater London, Wales and the West Midlands than in Northern regions.[16]

POVERTY WITHIN REGIONS

We have looked at inequalities between regions, but very often inequalities *within* regions are greater. In an analysis for the Rowntree Inquiry on Income and Wealth, Anne Green[17] looked at indicators of low income in 459 local authority districts and about 10,000 wards or neighbourhoods. On some measures Greater London as a whole was one of the richest regions, but Greater London boroughs such as Hackney and Tower Hamlets have some of the highest deprivation indicators. For example, in 1991, 62 per cent of households in Hackney or Tower Hamlets did not own a car. The differences *between* wards were found to be even greater than *between* local authority districts: while at a district level Hackney had the highest unemployment rate – over twice the national average – some ward districts in Liverpool were found to have unemployment rates more than four times the national rate.

Anne Green has demonstrated the extent to which there was a polarisation between poor and affluent ward areas between 1981 and 1991. Although those wards experiencing poverty in 1981 were broadly the same as those in poverty in 1991, the gaps between the 'best' and 'worst' wards increased. This increase in inequality was confirmed by a detailed study of Oxford and Oldham undertaken by researchers at the University of Oxford.[18] Using an index of deprivation indicators they showed that the poorest fifth of districts in Oldham had deteriorated between 1981 and 1991 while the

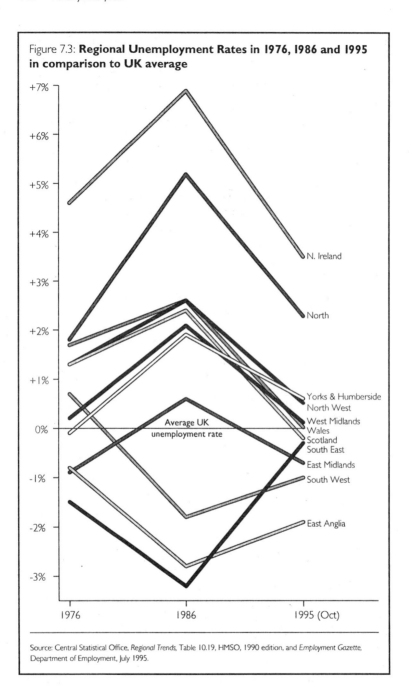

Figure 7.3: **Regional Unemployment Rates in 1976, 1986 and 1995 in comparison to UK average**

Source: Central Statistical Office, *Regional Trends*, Table 10.19, HMSO, 1990 edition, and *Employment Gazette*, Department of Employment, July 1995.

richest fifth had improved. Similar patterns were found in Oxford, although change had taken place at a much slower pace.

While it appears that a complex picture of poverty exists within regions, there are consistent themes within and across regions. Below we look at two striking themes: the plight of the inner city and the experience of rural poverty.

THE INNER CITY

In the ancient world, during the Middle Ages and Renaissance, even in the twentieth century, the word 'city' was frequently associated with wealth, success, culture and opportunity. The word 'civilisation' itself – and the word 'citizen' – derives from it. It is a bitter indictment of our own time that the phrase 'inner city' should today universally conjure up images of disorder, poverty, fear, vandalism and alienation.

(Susanne MacGregor and Ben Pimlott,
'Action and Inaction in the Cities')[19]

In recent years, the plight of the inner city has rarely been out of the headlines. The inner city has witnessed a number of economic and social changes: the exodus of manufacturing employment, the impoverishment of housing stock, public services which have borne the brunt of cuts and restructuring, rising crime rates and social division. There have been a number of studies which show that conditions in inner city areas have worsened despite government initiatives. Most recent among these is *Urban Trends 2: A decade in Britain's deprived urban areas,*[20] which builds on a previous report covering the years 1983-1991. The study confirms that England's urban areas are the most deprived in the country. Table 7.5 shows the proportion of people receiving supplementary benefit/income support in deprived areas – an important indicator of poverty. In all parts of the country the numbers receiving these benefits increased between 1983-85 and 1986-88, fell in 1989-91 and increased again in 1991-93. However, throughout the decade, the proportion of people receiving supplementary benefit/income support in the deprived areas was higher in each of the four periods than in England as a whole. In addition, the gap between the deprived areas and England generally has widened since 1983-85. The North West has continued to fare badly, with close to a third of people on supplementary benefit/income support since the mid-1980s. High levels of poverty have persisted in some London boroughs such as Hackney and Tower Hamlets.

TABLE 7.5: **Claimants receiving income support/supplementary benefit in deprived areas, people of all ages**

England	Percentages of estimated adult population			
	1983-85	1986-88	1989-91	1991-93
Brent	15.4	21.5	18.5	25.0
Greenwich	19.4	22.2	18.8	24.4
Hackney	29.5	39.7	32.4	37.6
Hammersmith & Fulham	20.8	24.8	20.0	20.8
Haringey	23.1	25.8	27.2	32.3
Islington	28.4	32.3	26.5	30.7
Kensington & Chelsea	17.5	22.1	15.9	16.8
Lambeth	27.4	32.3	28.9	29.4
Lewisham	21.5	24.9	22.1	24.2
Newham	24.4	27.4	27.3	35.8
Southwark	29.0	34.1	27.6	27.5
Tower Hamlets	34.7	38.3	32.6	34.2
Wandsworth	20.8	19.4	18.1	17.3
Greater London deprived areas	**23.5**	**27.6**	**24.4**	**27.1**
Knowsley	32.9	34.7	33.8	36.6
Liverpool	34.4	38.0	36.2	36.1
Manchester	22.2	34.2	32.0	34.8
Rochdale	22.0	20.3	16.2	19.5
Salford	25.0	25.7	22.3	24.3
North West Region five deprived areas	**27.0**	**32.3**	**29.8**	**31.8**
Birmingham	22.2	27.9	23.9	26.9
Coventry	23.1	24.3	19.3	20.5
Sandwell	25.6	26.0	20.2	22.8
Wolverhampton	24.7	27.4	21.9	24.4
West Midlands Region deprived areas	**23.3**	**26.9**	**22.4**	**24.8**
Bradford	21.3	21.2	18.5	21.7
All 23 deprived areas	**24.2**	**28.1**	**24.6**	**28.4**
England	**15.9**	**16.5**	**13.9**	**16.8**

Source: Supplementary Benefit/Income Support Quarterly Statistical Enquiries, reproduced from P. Willmott (ed), *Urban Trends 2, A decade in Britain's deprived urban areas*, Policy Studies Institute, 1994

Unemployment, lack of opportunities to train and social ghetto-isation of low income groups are often blamed for the low prosperity of inner city areas. In *Off the Map*, Mark Goodwin reminds us:

It is important to remember that this spiral is created and sustained by

broader sets of economic, social and political processes, whose origins
lay outside of the immediate urban sphere... It is easy to forget this
point, especially in the face of continuing political concern with an
'inner-city problem', which implies that such poverty is spatially
bounded and restricted to isolated pockets of deprivation.[21]

LONDON

As a capital city, London attracts a great deal of wealth, but it has
many of the features of inner city poverty.

In a study of deprivation in London, Peter Townsend found
substantial differences between dimensions of poverty in poor and
rich areas of the city.[22] He ranked 30 representative wards according
to levels of deprivation measured by unemployment, overcrowding
and the absence of ownership of a car or home. The most deprived
wards experienced substantially more material and social deprivation
than the least deprived wards. In a more recent study undertaken by
researchers at the University of Wales,[23] the most deprived and least
deprived wards in London were compared on four separate measures
(see Table 7.6). The study showed that the differences between the
least and the most deprived parts of the city in 1991 were extreme,
with up to eight times more people unemployed in the poorer wards
than in the richer wards. Thirty per cent of all households in the
poorest ward were suffering from overcrowding, compared to only
0.3 per cent in the least deprived; and up to 96 per cent of households
in the most deprived wards did not own their own home, compared
to only 3 per cent in the least deprived wards.

Different parts of London have very different rates of unemployment (see Table 7.7 and Figure 7.4).[24] Inner city Hackney and
Haringey had the highest unemployment rates in July 1995 – over
20 per cent according to official figures (over 30 per cent using the
Unemployment Unit index). On the whole, the outer London
constituencies had much lower rates of unemployment: the lowest
rates were in Richmond and Hillingdon at around 6 per cent using
the Unemployment Unit index. However, the gap between rich and
poor constituencies in London has narrowed because of the sharp
rise in unemployment which has hit the South East particularly hard
in the latest recession. In 1990, Hackney had an unemployment rate
of nearly six times that of Kingston; in 1995, it had dropped to three
and a half times.

TABLE 7.6: **Ranking of Greater London wards on measures of multiple deprivation – highest ranked ten wards and lowest ranked ten wards**

Ranked ward	Borough	Z-score index	Unemployed	Over-crowded	Not owning home	Percentage Not owning car
1. Spitalfields	Tower Hamlets	16.8	32.5	29.8	81.9	73.6
2. Liddle	Southwark	10.9	30.8	12.1	96.4	74.4
3. St Dunstan's	Tower Hamlets	10.8	27.4	16.2	83.8	68.6
4. St Mary's	Tower Hamlets	9.1	22.0	14.7	79.5	68.8
5. Weavers	Tower Hamlets	8.9	25.1	12.7	82.2	66.8
6. Shadwell	Tower Hamlets	8.9	22.6	15.8	78.4	58.1
7. Haggerston	Hackney	8.7	26.4	10.0	88.5	69.6
8. Holy Trinity	Tower Hamlets	8.5	25.2	12.0	80.7	65.0
9. Golbourne	Kensington & Chelsea	8.2	23.8	9.9	88.2	70.2
10. Kings Park	Hackney	8.1	27.6	8.2	89.2	67.5
755. Woodecote & Coulsdon West	Croydon	-5.6	4.7	1.3	10.1	12.2
756. Upminster	Havering	-5.8	4.1	0.6	6.9	17.6
757. West Wickham North	Bromley	-5.8	4.8	0.3	6.7	17.1
758. Crofton	Bromley	-5.9	4.2	0.5	5.5	17.1
759. Emerson Park	Havering	-5.9	5.1	0.8	5.3	12.6
760. Cranham West	Havering	-6.2	5.0	0.4	3.3	13.2
761. Biggin Hill	Bromley	-6.2	4.6	0.9	7.9	7.9
762. Cheam South	Sutton	-6.2	4.1	0.4	7.4	11.0
763. Selsdon	Croydon	-6.3	3.9	0.7	4.6	11.5
764. Woodcote	Sutton	-6.5	5.8	0.3	4.8	5.4

Source: OPCS, *1991 Census of Population* (OPCS, HMSO); data analysis conducted as part of ongoing research at the Department of Geography, University of Aberystwyth, as published in C Philo (ed), *Off the Map: the social geography of poverty in the UK,* CPAG Ltd, 1995.

TABLE 7.7: **Unemployment rates of London boroughs in July 1995 (percentages)**

	Dept of Employment Index	Unemployment Unit Index
Barking & Dagenham	11.1	16.2
Barnet	8.0	11.8
Bexley	7.5	10.9
Brent	15.5	23.1
Bromley	6.7	9.8
Camden	13.8	20.5
Croydon	9.7	14.2
Ealing	9.8	14.4
Enfield	10.0	14.7
Greenwich	13.0	19.0
Hackney	22.4	33.3
Hammersmith & Fulham	13.4	19.9
Haringey	20.5	30.5
Harrow	7.1	10.5
Havering	6.6	9.8
Hillingdon	6.2	9.0
Hounslow	9.2	13.5
Islington	17.3	25.5
Kensington & Chelsea	11.2	16.7
Kingston	6.4	9.4
Lambeth	18.9	28.0
Lewisham	16.2	23.9
Merton	9.6	14.1
Newham	18.5	27.2
Redbridge	9.1	13.3
Richmond	5.9	8.6
Southwark	18.8	27.7
Sutton	6.8	10.0
Tower Hamlets	19.6	23.9
Waltham Forest	14.2	20.8
Wandsworth	12.3	18.3
Westminster & City of London	10.7	16.0

Source: Unemployment Unit Briefing: *Unemployment totals & rates in parliamentary constituencies*, July 1995.

London also has larger inequalities in pay.[25] Although earnings in the capital are considerably higher on average than in the UK as a whole, the inequalities for male workers within London between the poorest and richest are far greater:

• The average wage for the poorest tenth of full-time male workers

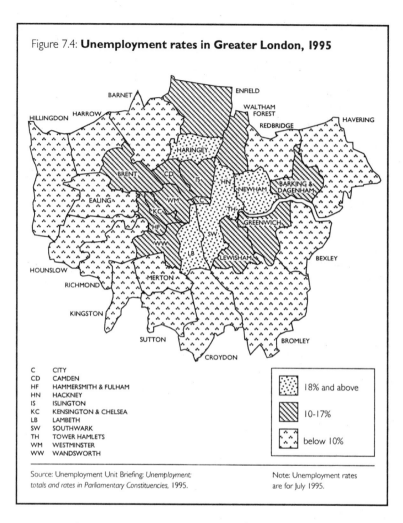

Figure 7.4: **Unemployment rates in Greater London, 1995**

C	CITY
CD	CAMDEN
HF	HAMMERSMITH & FULHAM
HN	HACKNEY
IS	ISLINGTON
KC	KENSINGTON & CHELSEA
LB	LAMBETH
SW	SOUTHWARK
TH	TOWER HAMLETS
WM	WESTMINSTER
WW	WANDSWORTH

18% and above

10-17%

below 10%

Source: Unemployment Unit Briefing: *Unemployment: totals and rates in Parliamentary Constituencies,* 1995.

Note: Unemployment rates are for July 1995.

was 55 per cent of the median wage (£384 per week) in Greater London and for the richest tenth it was 204 per cent of the median.

- The average wage for the poorest tenth of full-time male workers was 57 per cent of the median (£312.80 per week) in Britain and for the richest it was 186 per cent of the median.

RURAL POVERTY

The increasingly common assumption of countryside people as two-car-owning meritocracies can only serve to hide the plight of the non-mobile minority in gaining access to basic and necessary life-style opportunities.

(P Cloke *et al*, *Lifestyles in Rural England*,
Rural Development Commission, 1994)

It is estimated that a quarter of rural households live in or on the margins of poverty.[26] But, because poverty in rural areas is more dispersed, it is more hidden. Rural areas are undergoing substantial structural changes and poverty appears to be increasing. Rural areas have the lowest rates of pay in Britain. The Borders in Scotland comes at the bottom of the league, with male manual average weekly earnings at £224.30; Cornwall follows with £242.40, and then Dyfed in Wales with an average of £243.40.[27] The mainstays of employment such as farming and fishing have been decimated. For example, in June 1971 employment in agriculture, forestry and fishing stood at 421,000; by March 1995 this had fallen by 44 per cent to 233,400.[28] Wages in this sector are notoriously low. In April 1994:[29]

- the average gross weekly wage for full-time manual males in agriculture, forestry and fishing was £219.20 a week; 58.6 per cent earned below £220 a week compared to an average of 31.1 per cent for all industries;
- the average gross weekly wage for full-time manual females in agriculture, forestry and fishing was £169.80 a week; 58.8 per cent earned below £170 a week compared to an average of 52.6 per cent in all industries.

The Rural Development Commission's report into rural lifestyles[30] found that in nine out of 20 of the areas studied, 20 per cent or more of households were in or on the margins of poverty. There were some clear geographical variations – 39 per cent of Nottinghamshire households, 34 per cent of Devonshire households and 29 per cent of households in Essex were found to be in or on the margins of poverty, whereas relatively low levels of poverty were found in West Sussex, Cheshire and Northamptonshire. But, as the authors conclude, 'the juxtaposition of wealth and poverty merely heightens the relative impact of low income lifestyles in these supposedly better-off areas'.[31]

CONCLUSION

The geography of poverty is difficult to delineate. The broad brush approach to regional inequality masks vast differences both between and within regions. Despite cosmetic gestures towards urban renewal, inner cities present some of the starker images of poverty – homelessness, unemployment, cuts in public services and social polarisation. But poverty extends well beyond the towns and cities into the so-called rural idyll, where it is no less debilitating, even if it is less visible.

CPAG recognises the need for both local and national policies to reduce regional and local inequalities in living standards. We believe that central to a national anti-poverty strategy should be:

- investment in training and education;
- the introduction of employment initiatives to increase the availability of jobs;
- a national minimum wage;
- a national childcare strategy;
- an increase in benefit levels and the uprating of benefits in line with earnings or prices (whichever is higher) rather than prices alone;
- moves away from means-tested benefits towards a more inclusive social insurance system.

NOTES

1. C Philo, J McCormick and CPAG, '"Poor places" and beyond: summary findings and policy implications" in C Philo (ed), *Off the map: the social geography of poverty in the UK*, CPAG Ltd, 1995.
2. For attempts at drawing a map of poverty, *see* note 1; A Green, *The Geography of Poverty and Wealth*, Institute for Employment Research, 1994; D Gordon and R Forrest, *People and Places 2*, Saus, 1995.
3. *See* R Martin, 'Income and poverty inequalities across regional Britain: the North–South divide lingers on' in C Philo (ed), *see* note 1.
4. *See* note 2. See also M Noble *et al*, *Changing Patterns of Income and Wealth in Oxford and Oldham*, University of Oxford, 1994.
5. Central Statistical Office, *Regional Trends 30, 1995 edition*, Table 12.1, HMSO, 1995.
6. CPAG calculations derived from Department for Education and Employment and Welsh, Scottish and N. Ireland Offices data.
7. M Noble, G Smith *et al*, *Education Divides: poverty and schooling in the 1990s*, CPAG Ltd, 1995.

8. *See* note 7.
9. Central Statistical Office, *Family Spending. A report on the 1994/95 Family Expenditure Survey*, Government Statistical Service, HMSO, 1995.
10. *See* note 9.
11. V Borooah, P McKee and G Mulholland, 'Cost of living differences between the regions of the United Kingdom' in J Hills (ed), *New Inequalities: the changing distribution of income and wealth in the UK* (provisional title), Cambridge University Press, forthcoming.
12. A Goodman and S Webb, *For richer and poorer, the changing distribution of income in the United Kingdom 1961-91*, IFS commentary No 42, London: Institute for Fiscal Studies, 1994.
13. *See* note 2.
14. Department for Education and Employment, *Employment Gazette, August 1995*, and Department of Employment, *Employment Gazette, Historical Supplement, Employment Statistics*, October 1994, Vol 102, No 10.
15. Department for Education and Employment, *Employment Gazette*, August 1995.
16. Department for Education and Employment, *Employment Gazette*, August 1995, and Department of Employment, *Employment Gazette*, November 1992.
17. *See* note 2.
18. *See* note 4.
19. S MacGregor and B Pimlott (eds), *Tackling the Inner Cities: the 1980s reviewed, prospects for the 1990s*, Clarendon Press, 1991.
20. P Willmott, *Urban Trends 2, A decade in Britain's deprived areas*, Policy Studies Institute, 1994.
21. M Goodwin, 'Poverty in the city: you can raise your voice but who is listening?' in C Philo (ed), *see* note 1.
22. P Townsend, 'Living standards and health in the inner cities' in S MacGregor and B Pimlott (eds), *see* note 19.
23. *See* note 21
24. *See* note 15 and Unemployment Unit Briefing, *Unemployment totals and rates in parliamentary constituencies*, July 1995.
25. Department of Employment, *New Earnings Survey 1994*, Part E, Government Statistical Service, HMSO, 1994.
26. P Cloke, P Milbourne and C Thomas, *Lifestyles in Rural England*, Rural Development Commission, 1994.
27. Department of Employment, *New Earnings Survey 1994*, Part A, Government Statistical Service, HMSO, 1994
28. *See* note 14.
29. Department of Employment, *New Earnings Survey 1994*, Part A, Government Statistical Service, HMSO, 1994.

30. *See* note 26.
31. P Cloke, P Milbourne and C Thomas, 'Poverty in the countryside: out of sight and out of mind' in C Philo (ed), *see* note 1.

8 Poverty in Europe

... social exclusion is an endemic phenomenon ... It threatens the social cohesion of each member state and of the Union as a whole.
(European Social Policy White Paper, 1994)[1]

In 1988 nearly 52 million people[2] – 15 per cent of the population – in the European Union were living in poverty.[3] How does the United Kingdom compare with its European partners? This is not just an academic question. As a member of the European Union and in the context of a single European market, it is important to look at poverty in the UK in relation to other member states in order to assess how far we are experiencing common or differing trends, and to gauge the impact of a free market in Europe on our societies.

The countries of the European Union are very different, ranging from highly industrialised Germany to countries like Greece, Ireland, Portugal and Spain which have large agricultural sectors. There are also considerable disparities in wealth: Luxembourg has the highest per capita gross domestic product, and Portugal and Greece the lowest, in relation to the European average (see Table 8.1). These characteristics shape the nature of poverty in the different countries. There are also large differences within countries. For example, in 1992, in the southern region of Italy, the proportion of the workforce in agricultural work was 16.6 per cent, in comparison with 7.9 per cent in Italy as a whole. The gross domestic product per capita in this region is 72 per cent of the average for the European Union, while Italy as a whole has 106 per cent of the average for the European Union.[4]

TABLE 8.1: **European Union comparisons: gross domestic product (per head) in 1992**

Country	
European Union	100
Belgium	110
Denmark	108
France	113
Germany	108
Greece	50
Ireland	77
Italy	106
Luxembourg	131
Netherlands	103
Portugal	67
Spain	78
United Kingdom	99

Note: GDP per head is compared to the European Union average.

Source: Central Statistical Office, *Regional Trends 30*, Table 2.1, HMSO, 1995

PATTERNS OF POVERTY IN THE EUROPEAN COMMUNITY

The poor shall be taken to mean persons, families and groups of persons whose resources (material, cultural, social) are so limited as to exclude them from the minimum acceptable way of life in the Member State in which they live.

(Definition of poverty adopted in the Council Decision of 19 December 1984)

Since the late 1980s, the term 'social exclusion' has been most commonly adopted by the European Commission in relation to poverty, emphasising the processes by which people become poor.

Exclusion processes are dynamic and multidimensional in nature. They are linked not only to unemployment and/or to low incomes, but also to housing conditions, levels of education and opportunities, health, discrimination, citizenship and integration in the local community.

(*European Social Policy White Paper*, 1994)

However, there is as yet no European-wide operational definition of social exclusion and the term is frequently used with reference to issues far broader than those reflected by poverty statistics.[5]

The latest survey by Eurostat shows comparative rates of poverty in the European Union in 1988 (see Table 8.2).[5]

TABLE 8.2: **National poverty rates and numbers in the European Union in 1980 and 1988**

Country	Persons (poverty in figures methodology) 1980		Persons (poverty in figures methodology) 1988		Persons (poverty statistics methodology) 1988	
	%	Nos (000)	%	Nos (000)	%	Nos (000)
Belgium	7.1	701	8.4	832	7.4	729
Denmark	7.9	407	n/a	n/a	3.9	200
Germany	10.5	6,448	14.3	8,787	10.9	6,675
Greece	21.5	2,073	22.4	2,240	18.7	1,868
Spain	20.9	7,829	20.8	8,728	16.9	6,546
France*	19.1	10,313	19.4	10,894	14.7	8,234
Ireland	18.4	625	19.5	691	15.7	556
Italy	14.1	7,941	24.2	13,893	21.1	12,111
Luxembourg	n/a	n/a	16.0	59	11.1	41
Netherlands	9.6	1,363	8.5	1,253	4.8	706
Portugal*	32.4	3,167	27.9	2,728	24.5	2,525
United Kingdom	14.6	8,226	18.7	10,648	14.8	8,436

Note: The poverty line used is 50% of national average household expenditure adjusted for family size.

* Figures for 1989.

Source: Eurostat, *Poverty in Figures: Europe in the early 1980s*, Luxembourg: Office for Official Publications of the EC, 1990; Eurostat, *Poverty Statistics in the Late 1980s: research based on micro-data*, Luxembourg: Office for Official Publications of the EC, 1994.

Table 8.2 and Figure 8.1 set out the proportions and numbers of the population in poverty in each country. Poverty is defined as less than 50 per cent of the national average household *expenditure*, adjusted for family size.[7]

Two different methodologies have been used to calculate the figures. The most recent figures, for 1988 ('poverty statistics'), were calculated using more complete data than were available when the poverty figures for 1980 ('poverty in figures') were calculated. However, in order to be able to make a direct comparison between poverty levels in 1980 and 1988, figures calculated using the 'poverty in figures' methodology for 1988 are also given here.

Table 8.2 shows that in 1988:

- Portugal had the worst rate of poverty – nearly a quarter of its population was living in poverty;
- Italy, Spain and Greece followed with between 18.7 per cent and

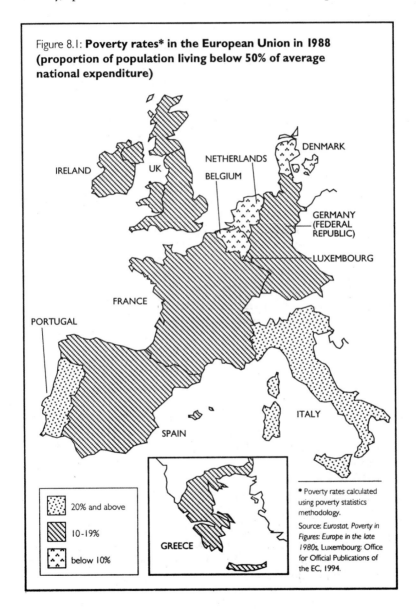

Figure 8.1: **Poverty rates* in the European Union in 1988 (proportion of population living below 50% of average national expenditure)**

Legend:
- 20% and above
- 10-19%
- below 10%

* Poverty rates calculated using poverty statistics methodology.

Source: *Eurostat, Poverty in Figures: Europe in the late 1980s*, Luxembourg: Office for Official Publications of the EC, 1994.

21.1 per cent of their population in poverty;

- of the more prosperous countries, the UK and France had the highest poverty rates at 14.8 per cent and 14.7 per cent respectively;
- Belgium, Denmark, Germany and the Netherlands had the lowest rates of poverty – between about 4 per cent and 11 per cent of the population.

Between 1980 and 1988, poverty rates increased in all EC countries, with the exception of the Netherlands, Portugal and Spain. During this period, Italy, Germany and the United Kingdom experienced the sharpest rises in poverty.

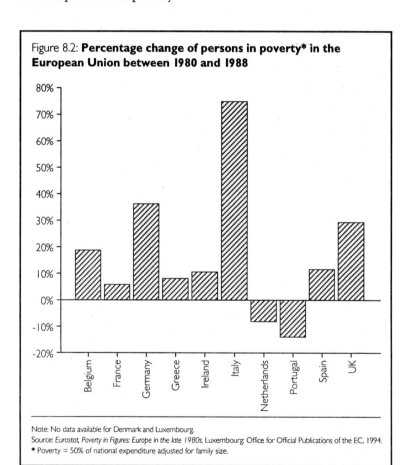

Figure 8.2: **Percentage change of persons in poverty* in the European Union between 1980 and 1988**

Note: No data available for Denmark and Luxembourg.
Source: Eurostat, Poverty in Figures: Europe in the late 1980s, Luxembourg: Office for Official Publications of the EC, 1994.
* Poverty = 50% of national expenditure adjusted for family size.

As Table 8.3, shows there are considerable differences between European Union member states in rates of child poverty. Portugal fares worst, with over one fifth of children under the age of 14 and one quarter of all 14–16 year olds living in poverty. Ireland and Italy also have a high proportion of children living in poverty. In the UK 18 per cent of children under 14 were living in poverty in 1988, according to the measure adopted by the European Commission.

TABLE 8.3: **Proportion of children living in poverty (poverty statistics methodology)**

	Age of children	
	<14	14–16
France 1989	16.0	19.4
Spain 1988	16.8	21.1
Portugal 1989	22.3	25.0
Italy 1988	19.5	22.7
Greece 1988	15.0	19.8
Ireland 1987	21.0	n/a
Belgium 1987/88	6.2	12.8
Luxembourg 1987	11.4	18.0
Denmark 1987	3.3	4.2
Netherlands 1988	4.3	3.9
UK 1988	18.5	14.5
Germany 1988	14.4	10.8

Source: Eurostat, Poverty Statistics in the late 1980s: research based on micro data. Luxembourg: Office for Official Publications of the European Communities, 1994

The methodology previously used to calculate poverty rates has been criticised as overestimating levels of poverty in the United Kingdom.[8] Nevertheless, recent calculations of poverty rates based on more complete data continue to indicate high levels of poverty in the United Kingdom compared to other European countries.

'NEW' POVERTY

The term 'new poverty' has been used to indicate the changing face of poverty in Europe. In 'New Poverty' in the European Community, Graham Room noted five aspects of 'new poverty': the rise in the numbers on social assistance; the growth of unemployment and insecure employment; the rise in bad debts and arrears; the increase in the number of lone parents and the number of homeless people. While the term 'new poverty' is not intended to imply that some 'old' types of poverty – among the elderly, children or the sick, for example – no longer exist, it focuses attention on those who are increasingly on the margins of society.[9]

ATTITUDES TO POVERTY IN THE EUROPEAN UNION

There has been an increase in awareness about the existence of poverty in Europe in the 1990s. Surveys conducted by the European Commission found that around three times more Europeans in 1993 reported situations of extreme poverty in their local area than in 1989 (13 per cent compared to 4 per cent).[10] There was also a substantial rise between 1989 and 1993 in the perception of the existence of people in danger of becoming poor (13 per cent to 37 per cent). The growth in awareness about the risk of poverty was found to be particularly significant in the UK.

In the 1990s, people are more likely to attribute poverty to injustice in society than to laziness or poor attitudes. The European Commission survey found that, in 1993, 11 per cent of those surveyed thought that poverty was the result of laziness or poor attitudes compared to 25 per cent in 1976.[11] In contrast, 39 per cent thought that poverty was the result of injustice in society in 1993 compared to 26 per cent in 1976.

In 1993, 79 per cent of people surveyed by the European Commission felt that the gap between the rich and poor was growing, compared to 70 per cent in 1989. Long-term unemployment is perceived as the most frequent cause of poverty and 14 per cent of those surveyed also reported that cuts in social protection were a common cause of poverty.

There appears to be a strong consensus on the need for public authorities to act to tackle poverty and social exclusion. Fifty-eight per cent of Europeans interviewed believed that global action is needed to combat poverty, particularly in the areas of employment, housing, education and social protection. Eighty per cent of Europeans consider that the public authorities are a prime 'player' with a duty to intervene in the fight against poverty. Even more Europeans (89 per cent) supported European Union intervention in this field.

A SOCIAL EUROPE?

It is still unclear what action will and can be taken in the foreseeable future to tackle growing levels of poverty at a European level. European social policy – once predicted by President Jacques Delors to be largely instigated by the European Commission, rather than member states themselves[12] – has yet to be fully developed or make any significant impact on the living standards of Europe's poor. As Lionel Barber, writing generally on European policy, has noted:

> The present posture of the member states and of the European Commission is to lower expectations and the political temperature.
>
> (*Financial Times*, 2 June 1995)

While the question of the future direction of European social policy, lies beyond the focus of this book,[13] it is possible to make a very brief assessment of EC action to tackle poverty to date, the impact of the Internal Market on poverty and the potential direction of future anti-poverty initiatives.

The 'social dimension' has consistently emphasised the need for improvements in living and working conditions and social and economic cohesion, but has been constrained by its focus on workers rather than citizens. Neither the Social Chapter nor Charter explicitly stated the eradication of poverty as a goal. Some action to tackle poverty has been taken via the Commission's Poverty Programmes (Poverty 1, 1975–1980; Poverty 2, 1986–1989; Poverty 3, 1990–1994). The Poverty Programmes have largely consisted of funding local, short-term, action-based projects. Particular emphasis has recently been placed on supporting partnership projects which develop interagency strategies and client participation, and offer services or new thinking which otherwise would not be supported locally. Poverty 3 (1990–1994) devoted 55 million ECUs (£46 million) towards supporting 30 local projects and 12 larger-scale initiatives.

The Poverty Programmes have been criticised for their limited scope. The House of Lords' Select Committee on the European Communities' report into Poverty 3, for example, described Poverty Programme support as 'a drop in the ocean'.[14] Nevertheless, their purpose has never been to eradicate poverty directly but to provide a catalyst for action at local and national levels by demonstrating what can be done. However, given rising levels of poverty in Europe, the effectiveness of the poverty programmes and the absence of binding legislation at a European level in the area of social policy need to be examined critically.

To some extent action at a European level may serve to increase levels of poverty rather than reduce them, at least temporarily. The introduction of a Single European Market has brought with it the threat of increased insecurity and marginalisation among certain communities. Concerns about 'social dumping', increased unemployment and downward pressure on wages have yet to be borne out in research findings.[15] However, the European Commission has acknowledged that some adverse consequences of economic integration are likely to be experienced by certain communities.

The UK's role in the development of European social policy has been characterised by stubborn resistance. The UK Government refused to sign the Community Charter of the Fundamental Social Rights of Workers (the 'Social Charter') and opposed the Social Chapter which was passed as a separate 'Social Protocol' as part of the Maastricht Treaty. The UK, among others, has also voiced resistance to Directives on parental leave and works councils (both withdrawn) and has sought to water down others (such as the 1992 'Pregnant Workers' Directive'). The continued intransigence of the UK over European social policy deprives workers and people in poverty of the benefit of progressive measures implemented elsewhere in the EC.

In the run-up to the revision of the Maastricht Treaty, the future of the European Union, its membership, goals and action is largely unknown. The future of European anti-poverty initiatives seems particularly unclear with the delay in the implementation of Poverty 4. The European Medium Term Social Action Programme (1995–1997) denotes 1996 as the year for the opening up of a European-wide debate on poverty and social exclusion as the basis for identifying the scope for concerted action. The House of Lords' Select Committee on the European Communities[16] has called for a coherent general policy framework to tackle social exclusion in Europe which might include targets for a reduction of the numbers living in poverty. In the absence of such a framework, there seems little doubt that significant levels of poverty in Europe will persist.

CONCLUSION

Poverty has risen in the United Kingdom more rapidly than most other European countries. As members of the European Union and in the context of a European Single Market, action to tackle rising poverty must take place at European as well as national levels, if it is to be effective.

CPAG believes that the European 'social dimension' should be strengthened by the UK:

- opting in to the Social Protocol to enable the UK to be covered by European Union decisions on social policy;
- endorsing action to bring forward European directives which would strengthen the support available for families with children (such as parental leave provisions and leave for family reasons);
- proposing draft directives on: the requirement on member states to establish a national minimum wage and a guaranteed national minimum income; minimum standards of provision for childcare services and moves to combat discrimination in social security against minority ethnic groups and against unemployed people;
- developing further research on poverty in European Union member states;
- supporting the creation of an all-party anti-poverty group in the European Parliament to monitor changes in poverty.

NOTES

1. *European Social Policy: a way forward for the Union, A White Paper*, European Commission, Directorate-General for Employment, Industrial Relations and Social Affairs, 1994.
2. This figure is derived from Eurostat's 'poverty in figures' methodology using OECD equivalence scales. Using Eurostat's 'poverty statistics' methodology, a figure of 49 million is derived.
3. Eurostat, *Poverty Statistics in the Late 1980s: research based on micro-data*, Luxembourg: Office for Official Publications of the European Communities, 1994. Poverty is defined as less than 50 per cent of national average household expenditure.
4. Central Statistical Office, *Regional Trends 29, 1994*, Table 2.1, HMSO, 1994.
5. For a fuller discussion of the term, see G Room (ed), *Beyond the Threshold: the measurement and analysis of social exclusion*, The Policy Press, 1995.
6. *See* note 2.
7. Previous studies have used 50 per cent of average income (adjusted for family size) as a poverty line. *See* M O'Higgins and Dr S Jenkins, 'Poverty in Europe: estimates for 1975, 1980 and 1985', unpublished paper, August 1989.

8. M Cross, *Parameters of Poverty, an overview of the UK in a European context*, Briefing Paper for Edinburgh Poverty Summit, December 1992.
9. G Room, *New Poverty in the European Community*, Macmillan, 1990; and G Room, 'A time for change', in S Becker (ed), *Windows of Opportunity: public policy and the poor*, CPAG Ltd, 1991.
10. N Rigaux, *The Perception of Poverty and Social Exclusion in Europe 1994*, Eurobarometer 40, European Commission DGV, 1995. For a discussion of Eurobarometer surveys, *see* Peter Golding, 'Public attitudes to social exclusion: some problems of measurement and analysis' in G Room (ed), *see* note 5
11. *See* note 10.
12. Speech to TUC, Bournemouth, 1988.
13. *See* R Dahrendorf, 'The new Europe', *Journal of European Social Policy*, 2 (2), 79-85, 1992; L Cram, 'Calling the tune without paying the piper? Social policy regulation: the role of the Commission in European Community social policy', *Policy and Politics*, 136-146, 1993; M Kleinman and D Piachaud, 'European social policy: conceptions and choices', *Journal of European Social Policy*, 3 (1), 1-19, 1993.
14. House of Lords' Select Committee on the European Communities, *The Poverty Programme*, HMSO, 1994.
15. See, for example, N Adnett, 'Social dumping and European economic integration', *Journal of European Social Policy*, 5 (1), 1-12, 1995.
16. *See* note 14.

9 Growing divisions

Neo-liberal policies have accelerated and aggravated powerful trends to inequality arising from changes in the world economy. These changes ... affect all industrial countries. But those where policies of deregulation and rolling back the welfare state have been most relentlessly applied are the places where inequality has grown most spectacularly.
(John Gray, Fellow of Jesus College, Oxford, *Guardian*,
17 February 1995)

For the first time since the Second World War the share of income of the poor is shrinking. The 1980s witnessed a widening gulf between rich and poor. The findings of the much publicised Rowntree Inquiry into Income and Wealth confirm the picture of a marked sharpening of inequality. They provide a rich source of material about the extent, causes and consequences of inequality which we draw upon in this chapter.[1]

Some believe that such a divide is irrelevant as long as overall standards of living improve. But for CPAG, along with many other organisations and individuals, such divisions scar our society.

INDICATORS OF DIVISIONS BETWEEN RICH AND POOR

INCOME INEQUALITY

Mr Blair: 'Does the Prime Minister accept it as a responsibility of government to reduce inequality?'
The Prime Minister: 'Yes'.
(House of Commons, *Hansard*, 9 February 1995, col 452)

The gulf that has opened between poor and rich is clearly demon-strated by analysis of the data in the government's *Households below Average Income* (HBAI) statistics.[2] Over the last decade, the incomes of the top and bottom of the population have been moving in opposite directions – a fall for the poorest and huge rises for the richest. As Table 9.1 shows, between 1979 and 1992/93, the poorest tenth of the population, including the self-employed,[3] experienced a *fall* in their real income of 18 per cent after housing costs, compared to a rise of 37 per cent for the whole of society and a staggering leap of 61 per cent for the top tenth.

TABLE 9.1: **Percentage changes in real income between 1979 and 1992/93 by decile group**

		%
Decile group	Income before housing costs	Income after housing costs
First (bottom)	0	−18
Second	8	0
Third	12	6
Fourth	16	15
Fifth	23	23
Sixth	28	29
Seventh	32	34
Eighth	36	39
Ninth	44	47
Tenth (top)	56	61
Total population (mean)	36	37

Note: Some figures are of less certain accuracy due to sampling error or the choice of equivalence scales.
Source: DSS, *Households below Average Income, a statistical analysis 1979-1992/93*, Government Statistical Service, HMSO, 1995.

The HBAI statistics also show changes in the overall shape of the income distribution between 1979 and 1992/93. Overall, incomes have increased, with the exception of the poorest. The income distribution has also become more dispersed. There has been a rise in the numbers in the lowest bands of equivalent income, a fall in the number in the middle and large increases in the number of people with higher incomes. The official data show how the poor became detached from the rest of society, and excluded from the short-lived prosperity of the 1980s.[4]

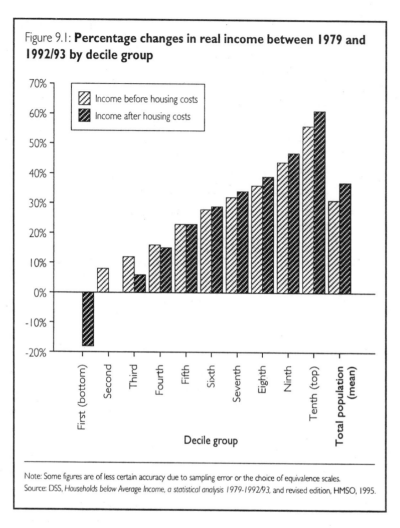

Figure 9.1: **Percentage changes in real income between 1979 and 1992/93 by decile group**

Note: Some figures are of less certain accuracy due to sampling error or the choice of equivalence scales.
Source: DSS, *Households below Average Income, a statistical analysis 1979-1992/93*, and revised edition, HMSO, 1995.

Not surprisingly, HBAI shows how between 1979 and 1992/93 the poorest half of the income distribution has seen its share of total income after housing costs drop from 32 per cent to 25 per cent, while the richest half increased its share from 68 per cent to 75 per cent.

Since the late 1970s, we have been witnessing the reversal of a long-term pattern. Having been stable since the Second World War, since the late 1970s the share of income of the poorer sections of society has been shrinking. It is no longer possible for the government to claim, as Mrs Thatcher did so confidently in 1988, that 'everyone in the nation has benefited from increased prosperity – everyone'.[5]

This trend is supported by rather different figures in *Economic Trends* which examine shares of total income.[6] These show that the earlier distribution from rich to poor has been put into reverse. The statistics reveal that in recent years household income has not trickled down but filtered up from the poorer sections of society to the richer ones.

TABLE 9.2: **Percentage distribution of total original and post-tax income of households, adjusted for family size, broken down into quintile groups (fifths)**

	1977 %	1979 %	1993 %
Quintile group		**Original income**	
Bottom	3.6	2.4	2.3
2nd	10	10	6
3rd	18	18	15
4th	26	27	25
Top	43	43	52
Quintile group		**Post-tax income**	
Bottom	9.4	9.5	6.6
2nd	14	13	11
3rd	17	18	16
4th	23	23	22
Top	37	37	44

Source: *Economic Trends, December 1994*, HMSO, 1994

Table 9.2 shows how the total amount of income held by households is distributed between the richest and poorest fifths of society. Two measures of income are used: 'original income' (ie, income before any taxes and benefits have been paid) and 'post-tax income' (ie, income after direct and indirect taxes and cash benefits). Both measures of income are adjusted for family size. Households are divided into fifths from bottom to top; these are known as *quintile groups*.

On both definitions of income, inequality has risen substantially between 1977 and 1993:

• the poorest fifth's share of total original income fell from 3.6 per cent to 2.3 per cent;

- the richest fifth's share of original income went up from 43 per cent to 52 per cent;
- the poorest fifth's share of all post-tax income has gone down from 9.4 per cent to 6.6 per cent;
- the richest fifth's share of all post-tax income has grown from 37 per cent to 44 per cent.

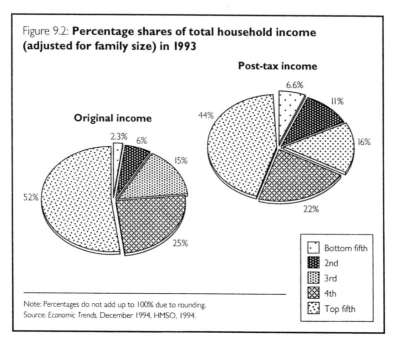

Figure 9.2: **Percentage shares of total household income (adjusted for family size) in 1993**

Post-tax income

Original income

Note: Percentages do not add up to 100% due to rounding.
Source: *Economic Trends*, December 1994, HMSO, 1994.

Legend:
- Bottom fifth
- 2nd
- 3rd
- 4th
- Top fifth

In fact, most of this shift from poor to rich occurred after 1979. The share of the top fifth in 1990 *after* taxes and cash benefits (44 per cent) is now slightly higher than it was in 1979 *before* any taxes and cash benefits had been paid.

EXPENDITURE INEQUALITY

Another way of looking at inequality is through *expenditure* rather than income. Each approach reveals different aspects of poverty or inequality. Tony Atkinson argues that a poverty line defined in terms of *income* is about a right to a minimum level of resources, while one which is defined in terms of *expenditure* is about a standard of living.[7] Each has strengths and weaknesses. Alissa Goodman and Steven

Webb conducted an analysis of changes in expenditure since 1979 which shows a substantial rise in expenditure inequality between 1979 and 1992.[8] However, this rise is not as substantial as the rise in income inequality. Table 9.3 shows the changes in expenditure before and after housing costs for the population broken down into tenths by income group (decile groups) between 1979 and 1992. There was a rise of 30 per cent in the real expenditure after housing costs for the bottom tenth (in contrast to a fall of 18 per cent in their income). There was a rise of 40 per cent in real expenditure after housing costs for the top tenth (the figure for the rise in income was 61 per cent). Figure 9.3 shows the different patterns for income and expenditure inequality after housing costs over the period between 1979 and 1992. (Note that the figures for income are slightly different from those given on page 167 as they are taken up to 1992, whereas the earlier figures are for 1992/93.)

TABLE 9.3: **Changes in income and expenditure (after housing costs) across the income distribution (1979-1992)**

Decile group	Income %	Expenditure %
First (bottom)	−18	30
Second	−1	7
Third	4	10
Fourth	13	15
Fifth	22	24
Sixth	28	25
Seventh	32	28
Eighth	39	29
Ninth	46	35
Tenth (top)	61	40

Source: Derived from A Goodman and S Webb, *The Distribution of UK Household Expenditure, 1979-1992*, Institute for Fiscal Studies, 1995

The authors suggest a number of possible explanations of why expenditure has risen for the poorest tenth while their income fell:

• The composition of the poorest tenth has changed. Pensioners, whose spending is low, have moved from the bottom tenth to higher up the income distribution. They have been replaced by unemployed people and families with children who tend to have higher spending patterns.

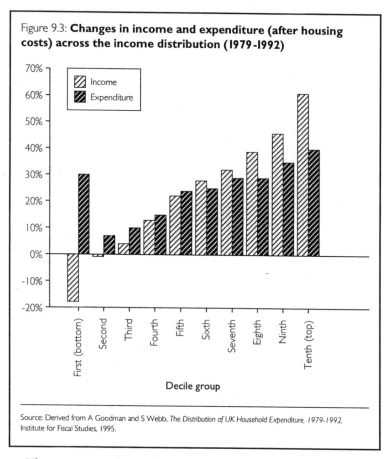

Figure 9.3: **Changes in income and expenditure (after housing costs) across the income distribution (1979-1992)**

Source: Derived from A Goodman and S Webb, *The Distribution of UK Household Expenditure, 1979-1992*, Institute for Fiscal Studies, 1995.

- The poorest tenth may be running down their savings in order to maintain their living standards. This is particularly true of those who have become unemployed and thus experienced a sudden change in their income.

- The poorest tenth may be getting into debt in order to maintain their living standards. While the analysis did not find a sharp increase in debt levels among this group, it used a narrow definition of debt, excluding forms of debt which tend to be high among poorer households. Moreover, families with children tend to have higher levels of debt.

- The growth in the number of self-employed in the bottom tenth, who tend to report low incomes but have high spending patterns, is reflected in the difference between income and spending results.

- The growth in the volatility of income is an important factor in an increasingly insecure labour market. Those who have experienced a rapid fall in their incomes may still have relatively high spending patterns.

PAY INEQUALITY

The male earnings distribution is now wider than at any time in the century for which we have records.

(John Hills, *Inquiry into Income and Wealth*)[9]

The last decade has been characterised by a substantial rise in earnings. However, the improvement of living standards for the average person masks a growing gap between the highest and lowest paid.[10]

- In 1978, the poorest tenth of men in full-time manual work earned 69 per cent of the average wage and the richest tenth earned 146 per cent.
- In 1993, the poorest tenth earned 63 per cent of the average wage and the richest tenth 159 per cent of the average.

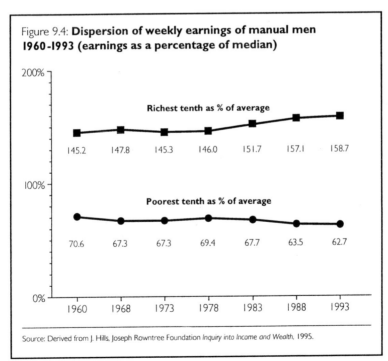

Figure 9.4: **Dispersion of weekly earnings of manual men 1960-1993 (earnings as a percentage of median)**

Richest tenth as % of average

145.2 147.8 145.3 146.0 151.7 157.1 158.7

Poorest tenth as % of average

70.6 67.3 67.3 69.4 67.7 63.5 62.7

1960 1968 1973 1978 1983 1988 1993

Source: Derived from J. Hills, Joseph Rowntree Foundation *Inquiry into Income and Wealth*, 1995.

Figure 9.4 shows how the pattern developed over 33 years. In the early 1970s earnings became less dispersed, but after 1976 the earnings of the lowest and highest paid grew steadily further and further apart.

WEALTH INEQUALITY

Wealth has to be distinguished from income. Unfortunately, shares of wealth are rarely discussed. Although inequalities in wealth have fallen markedly since the early sixties, the gulf between the poorest half of society and the top is still vast. Moreover, according to the Rowntree Report, the narrowing of the wealth gap stopped in the 1980s.[11] In 1992, the most wealthy 10 per cent of the population owned 49 per cent of the nation's marketable wealth, while the poorest half of the population owned a mere 8 per cent.[12] As Table 9.4 illustrates, patterns of wealth have remained stable since 1976.

TABLE 9.4: **Distribution of marketable wealth**[1]

	1976	1979	1986	1992
Most wealthy 1%	21	20	18	18
Most wealthy 10%	50	50	50	49
Least wealthy 50%	8	8	10	8

Note: 1. Marketable wealth excludes rights to state and occupational pensions

Source: *Inland Revenue Statistics, 1994*, Table 13.5, HMSO, 1994.

Owning your own home has become an increasingly important source of personal wealth. In 1992, two-thirds of people owned their own homes, compared to just over half (52 per cent) in 1979.[13] This striking change in patterns of tenure has had and will have far-reaching effects. Inheritance patterns will have a significant impact on some households in years to come as they will have no housing costs to speak of and thus a greater disposable income. For others on lower incomes or who have experienced insecurity in their jobs, home-ownership has proved to be an intolerable burden, leading to the sharp rise in repossessions. The expansion of owner-occupation has also had crucial consequences for the third of society who cannot afford to buy their own homes.

The polarisation in housing conditions is dramatically illustrated by Table 9.5 and Figure 9.5. They show the change in the work profiles of those in different tenures between 1979 and 1992/93.[14] The proportion of those in paid work fell for all tenure types; however, the trend was marked in the case of local authority/housing association accommodation. In 1979, 70 per cent of individuals in local authority/housing association accommodation were in paid work compared to 40 per cent in 1992/93. Thus, six out of ten people living in this sector were not in paid work in 1992/93. Unemployed people and people classified as 'other' – long-term sick and disabled people and non-working lone parents – now account for 37 per cent of people in local authority/housing association accommodation. The private rented sector shows broadly similar, though less marked, patterns, with a shift from those in work to the unemployed and 'other' categories.

TABLE 9.5: **Analysis of tenure by economic status 1979 to 1992/93**

		In work %	Head 60+ %	Unemployed %	Other* %
Owned outright	1979	58	35	2	5
	1992/93	43	49	3	5
Owned with mortgage	1979	95	2	1	2
	1992/93	89	3	4	4
Private rented	1979	72	18	3	6
	1992/93	61	14	10	16
LA/housing association	1979	70	17	5	8
	1992/93	40	23	16	21

Note: Percentages may not add up to 100% because of rounding.
*Other includes: long-term sick, disabled people and lone parents who are not in work.
Source: Calculated from DSS, *Households below Average Income, a statistical analysis 1979-1992/3*, HMSO, 1995

Polarisation between housing tenures ... has meant that those with the lowest incomes are becoming concentrated in the social rented sector and in particular neighbourhoods. The operation of the housing market is a key element in the cumulative disadvantage experienced by people living in particular localities.[15]

The third of society who are excluded from owning a home are forced to rely on a shrinking and impoverished public and privately

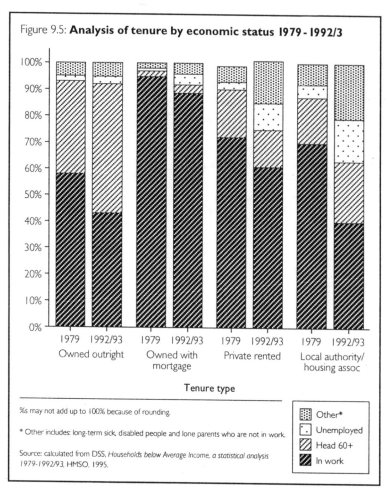

Figure 9.5: **Analysis of tenure by economic status 1979 - 1992/3**

Tenure type

%s may not add up to 100% because of rounding.

* Other includes: long-term sick, disabled people and lone parents who are not in work.

Source: calculated from DSS, *Households below Average Income, a statistical analysis* 1979-1992/93, HMSO, 1995.

Other*
Unemployed
Head 60+
In work

rented sector. However, there are also important divisions within the owner-occupied sector itself. The rising number of mortgage arrears and repossessions (see Chapter 4) is the outcome of a policy which has encouraged home-ownership among those on low incomes at a time of increasing insecurity in the labour market and decreasing government support for low income owner-occupiers.

The government's commitment to extending 'choice' is, in Fran Bennett's words:

prejudiced from the start by an allegiance to the inherently circumscribed principle of ownership. 'No principle is more crucial than what I call the "right to own",' said John Major – referring, in particular, to a home, shares and pensions. Those who can benefit from the 'opportunities' offered by tax relief on mortgage interest and private pension provision will, it appears, continue to do so – thus effectively blocking off one major route for the government to create a fairer distribution of resources and hence wider opportunities for all.[16]

TAXES AND GROWING INEQUALITY

Although social security is the principal instrument for reducing inequality taxation can play an important and independent role.
(D Mitchell, *Income Transfers in Ten Welfare States*)[17]

As the quotation above illustrates, social security and tax policies are important tools for either increasing or decreasing the scale of inequality.

There have been substantial reductions in income tax for people living on higher incomes, particularly in the 1980 and 1988 Budgets – the top rate of income tax has fallen from 83 per cent to 40 per cent. If the 1978/79 income tax system were in place today, £31.8 billion more tax revenue would be raised. Who has benefited from this £31.8 billion?

- The bottom 50 per cent of tax-payers have gained an average of £340 a year or £4.5 billion in total – 14 per cent of the total tax cuts.
- The top 10 per cent of tax-payers have gained an average of £6,000 a year, or £16 billion – half of the total tax cuts.
- The top 1 per cent of tax-payers at the very top end of the income distribution have gained an average of £35,800 a year, or £9.6 billion in total – under a third (30 per cent) of the total tax cuts.[18]

In their study of changes in taxation since 1985,[19] Christopher Giles and Paul Johnson found a number of broad trends:

- there has been a reduction in marginal rates of direct tax (income tax and national insurance), in particular for those on high incomes;
- there has been a shift towards indirect taxation (eg, raising VAT from 15 per cent to 17.5 per cent and extending it to fuel and the

increase of excise duties);
- there has been a widening of the tax base with the restriction of tax reliefs such as mortgage interest tax relief and the married couple's allowance.

Table 9.6 shows the broad impact of tax changes between 1985 and 1995.[20] The poorest four decile groups all lose on average from the changes, with the greatest losses in the poorest decile group who had an average loss of £3.00 per week or 2.9 per cent of their net income. Two-thirds of the poorest decile group were losers from the changes. In contrast, the top decile group gained an average of just over £31 a week or 5.8 per cent of their net income. Three-quarters of the top decile group were gainers. The shift from direct to indirect taxation has made the tax regime of 1995 significantly less progressive than that of 1985. The authors conclude:

the tax changes since 1985 have unambiguously increased inequality.[21]

TABLE 9.6: **Impact of tax changes, 1985-95, by decile group**

Decile	Average gain (£ per week)	Average gain (% of net income)	Percentage losing	Percentage gaining
1	–3.0	–2.9	66	7
2	–1.4	–1.4	44	13
3	–1.8	–1.5	47	23
4	–1.1	–0.8	43	40
5	0.7	0.4	37	50
6	1.6	0.7	33	57
7	3.1	1.2	29	64
8	4.4	1.5	25	69
9	6.3	1.8	23	72
10	31.3	5.8	20	76
All	4.10	1.70	37	47

Source: C Giles and P Johnson, 'Tax reform in the UK and changes in the progressivity of the tax system, 1985-95', *Fiscal Studies*, Vol 15, no 3, 1994

In addition, the authors examined the impact of the tax changes on different types of families (see Table 9.7). Families with children fare worst from the tax changes. Unemployed couples with children had an average weekly loss of £4.40 or 2.7 per cent of their net income, and lone parent families had a weekly loss of £1.60 or 1 per cent of their net income.

TABLE 9.7: **Proportions gaining/losing by family type**

Family type	Percentage losing	Percentage gaining	Average gain (£ per week)	Average gain (% of net income)
Single, unemployed	58	21	−1.1	−1.1
Single, employed	16	76	8.0	3.9
Single parent family	64	13	−1.6	−1.0
Unemployed couple, no children	53	31	0.1	0.1
Unemployed couple with children	78	8	−4.4	−2.7
One-earner couple, no children	44	46	5.3	2.1
One-earner couple with children	62	28	6.0	2.0
Two-earner couple, no children	28	65	6.0	1.7
Two-earner couple with children	46	47	4.7	1.3
Single pensioner	16	48	3.8	3.3
Couple pensioner	29	51	3.2	1.7
All	37	47	4.10	1.70

Source: C Giles and P Johnson, 'Tax reform in the UK and changes in the progressivity of the tax system, 1985-95', *Fiscal Studies*. Vol 15. no 3, 1994

INEQUALITY IN OTHER COUNTRIES

The UK is not alone in experiencing rises in inequality over the last decade and a half. The Rowntree Inquiry examined the changes in inequality in other industrialised countries.[22] It found that:

- greater inequality did not occur in *all* the industrialised countries over recent years; however, it did increase in most;
- the UK's level of income inequality was in the middle of the range of 11 industrialised countries;
- the rise in inequality in the UK was faster than in any other country for which there were comparable data, with the exception of New Zealand;
- the rise in the dispersion of earnings was a major cause of rising inequality in the USA, Canada and UK;
- the tax and benefit systems in Australia, Canada, France and Germany acted as a brake on growing market income inequalities, in contrast to those in other countries such as the UK, Sweden and the USA.

CONCLUSION

Over the 1980s increased earnings dispersion, higher unemployment, polarisation between two-earner and no-earner couples, rising self-employment and investment incomes, the declining relative value of cash benefits, and discretionary tax changes all pulled in the same direction, widening the gap between rich and poor households. Only a few factors – the rising importance of women's earnings relative to men's, and the 'automatic' effects of the tax system – pulled the other way.

(J Hills, *Inquiry into Income and Wealth, Volume 2*)[23]

There is no doubt that inequality, however measured, has increased dramatically over recent years. The causes of that rise, as highlighted by the quotation above, are complex and interrelated.

Even after tax and benefits and family size are taken into account, in 1992 the poorest fifth held just 6.6 per cent of all post-tax household income; the richest fifth held nearly seven times as much – 44 per cent. Changes in taxation and social security policies have brought a *declining* share of the national income to the poor and a *rising* share to the affluent. Inequality matters because the lifestyle of the rich and the array of goods they consume create a culture of affluence which locks out the poor. Social policies are reinforcing divisions and the exclusion experienced by the people who are living in and on the margins of poverty. The task of tackling inequality lies in many different areas of policy. A more progressive tax system, an employment and training strategy which puts unemployment at the forefront, a statutory minimum wage and more generous benefits would begin to address some of the inequalities that beset our society.

For Conservatism is grounded in fairmindedness, a sense of what is right; in shared aspirations and mutual respect. It builds on self-respect, not envy. It seeks to unite, and not to divide. To create ... a Britain without barriers.

(Rt Hon J Major, Speech to the Conservative Women's Conference, 27 June 1991)

Despite John Major's appeal for a united nation, rich and poor are more sharply divided than ever.

NOTES

1. J Hills, *Inquiry into Income and Wealth Vol 2*, Joseph Rowntree Foundation, 1995.
2. DSS, *Households below Average Income, a statistical analysis 1979-1992/93*, and revised edition, HMSO, 1995.
3. If the self-employed are excluded the figures show a small rise of 4 per cent for the poorest tenth before housing costs and a fall of 10 per cent after housing costs. *See* note 2.
4. *See* note 3.
5. House of Commons, *Hansard*, 17 May 1988, col 796.
6. *Economic Trends, December 1994*, HMSO, 1994.
7. A B Atkinson, *Poverty and Social Security*, Harvester Wheatsheaf, 1989.
8. A Goodman and S Webb, *The Distribution of UK Household Expenditure, 1979-92*, Institute for Fiscal Studies, 1995.
9. *See* note 1.
10. *See* note 1.
11. *See* note 1.
12. *Inland Revenue Statistics 1994*, HMSO, 1994.
13. OPCS, *General Household Survey 1993*, Government Statistical Service, HMSO, 1995.
14. *See* note 2, appendix 7.
15. P Lee, A Murie, A Marsh and M Riseborough, *The Price of Social Exclusion*, National Federation of Housing Associations, 1995.
16. F Bennett, 'A window of opportunity', in S Becker (ed), *Windows of Opportunity: public policy and the poor*, CPAG Ltd, 1991.
17. D Mitchell, *Income Transfers in Ten Welfare States*, Studies in Cash & Care, SPRU, Avebury, 1991.
18. House of Commons, *Hansard*, 10 December 1993, col 400.
19. C Giles and P Johnson, 'Tax reform in the UK and changes in the progressivity of the tax system, 1989-95', *Fiscal Studies*, Vol 15, No 3, pp 64-86, Institute for Fiscal Studies, 1994.
20. In the 1993 Budget, the Chancellor of the Exchequer announced the extension of VAT to fuel (which had previously been zero rated) at a rate of 8 per cent in April 1994 and going up to 17.5 per cent in April 1995. Following widespread opposition, the government was forced to agree that VAT on fuel should remain at 8 per cent. This analysis assumes that VAT is raised to 17.5 per cent on fuel as was the initial intention of the government. As a result, the figures slightly exaggerate the losses at the bottom, although the broad patterns remain the same.
21. *See* note 20.
22. *See* note 1.
23. *See* note 1.

Conclusion

Poverty blights the lives of around a quarter of the United Kingdom's population and a third of its children. It is evident in rural as well as urban areas – in the rural 'idyll' and the inner city. Here we have shown how levels of poverty in the UK have increased in comparison with other European countries and the extent to which income inequality has risen more rapidly in the UK than throughout almost all the industrialised world. We have shown how poverty excludes millions from full participation in society and endangers their health and homes. We have exposed the way in which the dice are loaded against millions of children, denying them the opportunity to fulfil this potential.

Poverty is often created when the tie to the labour market is severed – because of unemployment, or caring for another person at home, or disability. But access to the labour market does not in itself guarantee escape from poverty. Often, employment provides only low, insecure or sporadic earnings. Poverty is also intensified when the extra costs of having a child, coping with a disability or caring for an elderly relative are not met adequately by earnings or social security benefits. Such poverty is not random but shaped by class, by gender and by race. Policies to tackle poverty have to respond to several challenges:

- **demographic pressures** – the greater numbers of elderly, and especially very old people with greater disabilities;
- **economic changes** – higher unemployment, changing work patterns, low wages, growing inequality, and the concentration of poverty among Black and other ethnic minority communities;
- **social changes** – shifting patterns of family life, especially the

increase in the proportion of women with children in paid work and the rise in the number of lone parents;

- **a crisis of confidence** in the capacity of the welfare state to deal with poverty.

Grappling with these challenges has to take place against the background of a social security system which seems to have lost its way. Some, including the government, suggest that the social security system is no longer economically sustainable in its current form.[1]

Beveridge's post-war vision of social security to meet people's needs from cradle to grave has been severely undermined both by changes in society and by specific policies. The mainstay of Beveridge's social security scheme was national insurance: those in full-time paid work (largely men and single women) were to be catered for during interruptions to their work (unemployment, sickness, etc) and after retirement. Others (women and children) were to be provided for as 'dependants' of the male breadwinner. But such a model no longer fits reality.[2] Policies have weakened or abolished some key benefits and have withdrawn certain rights by, for example, freezing child benefit between 1988 and 1990, replacing invalidity benefit with incapacity benefit in April 1995 and introducing the jobseeker's allowance in October 1996. Over the last ten years, the marked shift towards means-testing in conjunction with the rise in unemployment has brought staggering numbers into the maze of means-testing, with its complexity, discretion, and delays. The ability of some parts of the social security system to function adequately has been called into question.

While there is a very good case for reforming the social security system, CPAG believes that the objectives for reform should not be driven by the sole criterion of reducing expenditure.[3] Rather, the rise in poverty and inequality in recent years should be the starting point for change. Lack of action to tackle growing poverty and inequality will only increase social security expenditure further. Action outside the social security system, via an effective employment strategy and progressive taxation measures, for example, will both reduce poverty and, correspondingly, expenditure on social security.

Policies to tackle poverty must also reflect a changes at a European level. The social and economic consequences of the single market in the European Union are as yet unrevealed and yet potentially more far-reaching than other economic changes experienced up to now. They bring the threat of increased inequalities, not only between countries in Europe, but also within countries themselves. The 'social dimension' of Europe is at present but a pale counterpart of the economic dimension. The protocol of the Maastricht Treaty, which embodies the 'social dimension', has been side-lined; and the UK stubbornly refuses to sign it. As we approach the revision of the Maastricht Treaty, and in the light of all these changes, what kind of strategy should we be pursuing in the United Kingdom to prevent poverty?

First, it must be a comprehensive strategy. The task of tackling poverty lies in many different areas of government – in policies for industry and the regions, for housing, education, social services and transport, and for the environment and energy, as well as in the traditional areas of employment, social security and taxation. We touch only briefly on the broader areas here. We focus on three principal tools for tackling poverty and redistributing resources:

- improving access to the labour market and conditions within it;
- improving the benefits which support those who are either not in paid work or who work part time;
- making the tax system fairer.

Employment, social security and taxation policies are the central tools for sharing out resources more fairly between rich and poor, healthy and sick, white people and Black people, employed and unemployed, able-bodied and disabled and between men and women.

> The wages, social security and tax system should, together, ensure that all members of society have sufficient income to enable them to meet their public and private obligations as citizens and exercise effectively their legal, political and social rights as citizens.
>
> (*Charter for Social Citizenship*)[4]

As the pages of *Poverty: the facts* reveal, poverty denies people the chance of achieving their potential. Thus, the framework for any anti-poverty policy must be to give people the bricks with which to build their future and the future for their children. These bricks include: a decent home, a comprehensive and free health system, free education, subsidised childcare, cheap public transport, an insulation and energy saving programme, and a healthy ·environment. More specifically, CPAG urges active steps towards the following policies.[5]

EMPLOYMENT

Work is central to our lives. Paid or unpaid it is the way in which we meet needs, create wealth and distribute resources. It is a source of personal identity and individual fulfilment, social status and relationships. It is the heart of wealth and welfare.

(Social Justice: Strategies for National Renewal)[6]

Formulating a strategy for employment lies at the heart of policies to reduce poverty. Employment policies should be about access to employment, about ensuring both flexibility and security for the workforce, about promoting anti-discrimination in employment and about preventing poverty at work. Such policies should include:

- Employment rights which apply equally to full- and part-time workers, including a statutory minimum wage.
- Provisions to enable women and men to combine paid work with caring responsibilities at home – increased access to childcare facilities for both under school age and schoolaged children which provide a stimulating environment for children; equal pay for women and men.
- Access to decent jobs and training for all, especially groups who experience discrimination in employment – women, Black people and other minority ethnic groups, unskilled workers, people with disabilities and long-term unemployed people.
- Endorsement of the European draft directives which improve the rights of parents and women at work – parental leave and leave for family reasons and pro rata rights for part-time and temporary workers.

SOCIAL SECURITY

If social security benefits are to reflect genuinely the risks and pressures in our modern and complex society, they should be capable of meeting a wider range of 'needs' than simply providing a residual safety net for the poor. In particular, if social security is to be a mechanism for preventing poverty or reducing inequalities significantly, benefits must be available *before* people become poor. It is not simply that it is in the best interests of individual claimants, it also builds a social security system based on the values of social solidarity and mutual support. The alternatives are more divisive, setting benefits recipients apart from the rest of society.[7]

The principles which should underpin social security are:

- Solidarity – collective security against risks, such as unemployment or sickness.
- The sharing by society as a whole of the responsibility for caring for children, elderly people and people with disabilities.
- Preventing poverty, rather than patching over it.

These principles mean a social security system which would provide:

- Adequate benefits to meet people's needs – physical, social and cultural – to enable people to participate fully in society. Benefits should be paid as far as possible without means tests.
- Individual autonomy – benefits paid on an individual basis so that women as well as men can claim benefits in their own right.
- Equal access and treatment regardless of sex, race, marital status or sexual orientation.
- Clear rights to benefits, which should be administered efficiently and humanely by sufficient staff.
- Simplicity – benefits should be easy to understand and administer.
- Flexibility – benefits should be paid in a way which includes those working part time within the social security system and in a way which takes account of cultural differences.

Above all, it is essential that the social security system caters for everyone rather than just people in poverty. This means moving away from the means test, rather than further strengthening its role. This is the only way to guarantee that social security does not become a second-class service for the most vulnerable.

> We are only likely to be able to meet the needs of the weak and vulnerable – which may include all of us at different points of our lives – if services recognise their special needs and do not push them to the margins of society. In justifying this conclusion, we must return once again to the basic truths which we believe must underlie any system of welfare. It must be concerned with the well-being of all members of society: the notion of interdependence and concern for the poor and oppressed demands no less. Any model which splits off the least fortunate members of society and treats them in a way which is fundamentally different from the rest is unacceptable.
>
> (*Not just for the Poor*)[8]

TAXATION

> Income, wealth and social welfare are unequally distributed in all OECD countries, and redistribution is an objective of society and the State ... There is a well-established role for the welfare state which is firmly rooted in the idea of market failure and the desire for redistributional justice.
>
> (*Social Expenditure 1960-90*)[9]

Taxation policies determine how much income people can keep out of their earnings or benefits and they are one of the principal means of redistributing income and wealth from rich to poor. Fairer policies on taxation should include:

- creating a more progressive tax structure;
- fully independent taxation for men and women, which does not depend on marital status;
- a local tax system which reflects ability to pay.

As well as these broad policies, CPAG believes that it is essential for governments to commit themselves to:

- research into people's basic physical and social needs in order to provide a rationale for adequate benefits;
- publishing annual statistics on low incomes which include a breakdown by region, gender and ethnic origin.

Only then will all governments be compelled publicly to recognise the existence of poverty and develop policies to combat it. As inequalities have grown and poverty has become more pressing and more intense, there has been strong public support for policies which tackle these injustices. The 1995/96 *British Social Attitudes Survey* revealed that in 1994:

- 56 per cent thought that the better-off should pay more in taxes;
- 58 per cent thought that government should spend more on benefits for the poor even if this meant higher taxes.[10]

An earlier *British Social Attitudes Survey* shows that nearly two-thirds support action to reduce income differences.[11] Such surveys reveal that the welfare state retains enduring popularity, despite cuts and changes. It has become fashionable to argue that the problems of poverty, low pay and unemployment can only be tackled after the development of a strong and stable economy – that to put concerns about poverty before economic development is to put the cart before the horse. However, CPAG is convinced that long-term economic growth must go hand in hand with social justice: that only a society which is not wracked by social division and the exclusion of the poor can provide the foundations for stability and growth. It has recently become equally fashionable to argue that redistribution has reached its limits; that taxation cannot be increased and that benefits will have to be means-tested or hived off to the private sector to reduce the bill to a level acceptable to the better-off. Yet this approach ignores the increase in unemployment that has created in large part the increase in social security expenditure – however inadequate it is. Prevention is better than picking up the pieces. But failure even to pick up the pieces – via benefits, jobs and services – is an abnegation of responsibility.

We need to build on the attitudes expressed in opinion surveys above. We need to point out that the 'modern' recipe of privatising provision where possible and means-testing the rest would result in a general reluctance to finance social welfare, the blunting of individual aspirations by increasing the number of people in the poverty trap and the paring back of provision for the poor. We would indeed be left with a 'residual' welfare state.

Each step upwards in the unemployment figures means an ever larger pool of long-term unemployed and yet more young people facing a jobless and poverty-stricken future. It is this divide between those in well-paid, secure jobs and those who are marginalised – either without work or in intermittent low-paid jobs – which poses the challenge for policy makers, political parties, the general public and, above all, for government.

> It is only so far as poverty is abolished that freedom is increased.
> (Harold Macmillan, *The Middle Way*)[12]

NOTES

1. Department of Social Security, *The Growth of Social Security*, HMSO, 1993.
2. See L Harker, *A Secure Future? Social security and the family in a changing world*, CPAG Ltd, 1996.
3. See C Oppenheim, *The Welfare State: putting the record straight*, CPAG Ltd, 1994.
4. R Lister, *The Exclusive Society: citizenship and the poor*, CPAG Ltd, 1990.

5. These policies come from a variety of sources, in particular from R Lister, *There is an Alternative*, CPAG Ltd, 1987; and the 'Charter for Social Citizenship' in R Lister, *The Exclusive Society: citizenship and the poor*, CPAG Ltd, 1990.

6. *Social Justice: strategies for national renewal*, the report of the Commission on Social Justice, Vintage, 1994.

7. *CPAG's submission to the Commission on Social Justice*, CPAG, 1994.

8. *Not Just for the Poor: Christian perspectives on the welfare state*, Church House Publishing, 1986.

9. *Social Expenditure 1960-1990*, OECD, 1985.

10. R Jowell et al (eds), *British Social Attitudes, the 12th report, 1995/96 edition*, SCPR, Dartmouth, 1995.

11. R Jowell et al (eds), *British Social Attitudes, special international report, 6th report*, Social and Community Planning Research, Gower, 1990.

12. H Macmillan, *The Middle Way*, 1962.

POVERTY LINES

We have looked at two sources of information to estimate the numbers living in poverty and the changes in their incomes: *Low Income Families* statistics (LIF) and *Households below Average Income* (HBAI). However, neither measure of poverty is entirely satisfactory; both have strengths and weaknesses.

LIMITATIONS OF THE STATISTICS

Both sets of statistics have three weaknesses in particular. First, they provide only a snapshot; they do not show how long people have been living in poverty – which could be a month or several years. Different groups might be more or less likely to experience long-term poverty. Such material can only be provided by longitudinal data (such as from the British Household Panel Survey). Secondly, they underestimate poverty because they are based on the Family Expenditure Survey (which excludes the homeless and those living in institutions) and they disregard the costs of being poor (eg, having to buy poor quality goods which do not last long or having to use local shops which are more expensive). Thirdly, they are predominantly based on income rather than expenditure and (although HBAI now includes some material on spending) thus do not reveal much about people's actual living standards.

USING INCOME SUPPORT AS A POVERTY LINE DERIVED FROM LOW INCOME FAMILIES STATISTICS

ADVANTAGES

- Income support is a minimum level of income set by Parliament for people not in 'full-time' work who meet certain conditions. It allows us to measure incomes in relation to this minimum level and thus judge how effective the government is in ensuring that people do not fall below it and that they are given the resources to rise above it.
- LIF uses the 'benefit assessment unit' (see Appendix 2) as the unit

of measurement rather than the 'household' (as is used by HBAI). More than one benefit unit may live in a single household. For example, if a lone-parent family on income support shares with a relative or friend who is on an average income, the lone-parent family is still counted as having a low income despite the higher income of the relative or friend. This reflects the assumption that income is not always shared equally within households. CPAG believes that the best unit of measurement is the individual; but the 'benefit unit' is closer to the 'individual' than the 'household' is. Thus, on the whole, the 'benefit unit' is a more appropriate unit of measurement than the 'household'.

DISADVANTAGES

- These are not official figures but have been produced by the independent Institute for Fiscal Studies for the House of Commons Social Security Committee.
- There is a difficulty with using income support both as a measure of poverty and as the tool to relieve poverty. Each time it is raised in real terms (ie, above inflation) to improve the living standards of the poorest, the number of people defined as poor is automatically increased. If income support was reduced by half, the numbers living in poverty would also be halved.
- Income support's level and coverage are determined by overall government priorities, rather than being related to people's needs. Thus, by using a benefit level as a poverty line, the anomalies in the benefit itself are mirrored in the way poverty is measured – eg, young people aged 18-24, who are single and childless, receive a lower rate of income support than those aged 25 and over. This is not necessarily a reflection of need and means that the poverty line is higher for those aged 25 and over than for those below 25.

USING 50 PER CENT OF AVERAGE INCOME AS A POVERTY LINE DERIVED FROM HOUSEHOLDS BELOW AVERAGE INCOME

ADVANTAGES

- These are official figures published by the government.
- They provide the only set of continuous data since 1979.

- It is an unapologetically 'relative' poverty line (see Chapter 1) which looks at low incomes in relation to the incomes of the rest of society. It rises and falls as average income rises and falls.

DISADVANTAGES

- 50 per cent of average income does not relate incomes to the minimum rates of benefit specified by Parliament – income support. This means we cannot judge the government by its own standards.
- The figures are based on the *household* unit rather than the benefit unit, as was used in the LIF figures. Using the *household* unit leads to a substantial *underestimate* of the number of people living on a low income. The DSS estimates that in 1992/93 the numbers falling below 50 per cent of average income after housing costs would be *1.5 million higher* (some 15.6 million people) using the *benefit unit* as the unit of measurement rather than *households*.[1]
- Some people would argue that 50 per cent of average income measures inequality rather than poverty.
- The 'average' may fluctuate from year to year for either statistical reasons or economic ones. For example, if average income fell drastically, say as a result of an oil-shock induced recession, the number of people below 50 per cent average income (and thus in 'poverty') would also fall, even though many of those on low incomes may actually be worse off.
- The equivalence scales (which are used to adjust income for family size) used in HBAI, known as the McClements scales, have lower weights for children than the equivalence scales used in LIF. This affects both the overall total and the composition of those in poverty. Research by the IFS has shown:

The choice of scale makes a substantial difference to the recorded extent and make-up of poverty and inequality. In recent years, increasing the weight given to children increases the numbers recorded as living 'in poverty' (living on below half average income). Decreasing the weight given to them reduces recorded poverty numbers. Using the income support scales in constructing poverty statistics would therefore show greater recorded poverty than is found using the McClements scales.[2]

The list of advantages and disadvantages makes it abundantly clear that there is no straightforward answer to finding an uncontroversial poverty line. We have chosen to use both the LIF and HBAI, drawing out the strengths of each analysis.

NOTES

1. DSS, *Households below Average Income, a statistical analysis 1979–1992/93*, Government Statistical Office, HMSO, June 1995, and revised edition, October 1995.
2. J Banks and P Johnson, *Children and Household Living Standards*, Institute for Fiscal Studies, 1993.

APPENDIX 2

DEFINITIONS AND TERMS

Average is a single number that is intended to be representative of a set of numbers. There are different kinds of averages – means, median and mode. In *Poverty: the facts* only the mean and median are used. The **mean** is when all the numbers are added up and then the total is divided by the number of numbers. The **median** is the mid-point of any range of numbers. The mean is less stable than the median as it tends to become unrepresentative if it is dragged up by a few very large or small numbers. In the government's *Households below Average Income* figures, people's incomes are measured as a proportion of the mean income.

Benefit Assessment Unit is an individual or couple, with or without children, on which entitlement to supplementary benefit or income support is based (*see* Low Income Families).

Child – in the government figures, *Households below Average Income* and *Low Income Families*, a child is defined as anyone aged under 16, or 16-19 if s/he is in full-time, non-advanced education.

Council tax benefit covers 100 per cent of the council tax for those living on income support or an equivalent level of income. It replaced community charge benefit from April 1993.

Decile groups – successive tenths of all households arranged by income from bottom to top.

Equivalence scales are used to adjust income to take account of different family or household sizes. This is done in order to reflect the extent to which families or households require different incomes to achieve the same standard of living. For example, a two-parent family with two children has an income of £200 a week. Assuming that a couple has a weight of 1.00 and each child 0.50, when income is **equivalised**, it is £100 a week (£200 divided by 2.00). There is a great deal of controversy about which equivalence scales are appropriate – eg, how much weight to place on children's needs at different ages. The government's *Households below Average Income* statistics use different equivalence scales from those used in *Low Income Families*.

Family credit is a means-tested social security benefit for families with children in low-paid work (for 16 hours a week or more). It replaced family income supplement as part of the 1986 Social Security Act (fully implemented in 1988).

Family Expenditure Survey is conducted annually by the Central Statistical Office. The *Family Expenditure Survey* is a survey of people's expenditure and income in the United Kingdom.

Households below Average Income (HBAI) was produced by the Department of Social Security for the first time in 1988 and has replaced the *Low Income Families* statistics. HBAI is based on an analysis of the *Family Expenditure Survey*. HBAI measures the numbers of people living on incomes below the average (the mean). The HBAI figures are for the United Kingdom. HBAI uses **household** income which is adjusted for household size (equivalised) and then divided by the numbers of individuals in the household. Income is current (ie, the income stated at the time of the **Family Expenditure Survey** interview). Income is defined as: net earnings after income tax, national insurance and occupational pension contributions, gross profit from self-employment, all social security benefits including housing benefit, maintenance, investment income, and some income in kind, such as luncheon vouchers and free school meals. Income is net of the following items: income tax payments, national insurance contributions, contributions to occupational pensions, domestic rates, council tax and repayments of social fund loans. The statistics show income before and after housing costs. Housing costs are defined as: rent and rates, water rates, ground rent and service charges, mortgage interest and structural insurance for home owners. CPAG argues that one possible poverty line is 50 per cent of average income after housing costs.

Housing benefit is a means-tested social security benefit which helps people on low incomes in and out of work with their housing costs.

Income can be measured in a number of different ways. See *Households below Average Income* and *Low Income Families* for definitions used in these series. In Chapter 9, figures are used from the government's Central Statistical Office publication, *Economic Trends*. We have picked out two measures of income: original income (ie, income before taxes and benefits) and post-tax income (ie, income after direct taxes such as income tax and national insurance and indirect taxes, ie VAT and cash benefits).

Income support is a social security benefit which is supposed to provide a minimum income for people who are not in 'full-time' work (ie, work less than 16 hours a week) who meet certain conditions. It is means-tested. It replaced supplementary benefit as part of the 1986 Social Security Act (implemented in 1988) – *see* Social Security Act 1986. Income support and its predecessor, supplementary benefit, are often regarded as the 'safety net' of the social security system; they were intended to provide a kind of minimum income guarantee. However, the government has deliberately excluded some groups from income support through rules on full-time work, or capital, or age. Thus, increasingly, income support is becoming a far less effective safety net.

Institute for Fiscal Studies is an educational charity which promotes research and discussion of tax and finance matters. It has undertaken a great deal of work on behalf of the House of Commons Social Security Committee in looking at the distribution of low income.

Lone parents – throughout the text we use lone parents to refer to anyone who is bringing up children on their own whether they are divorced, separated, widowed or never married.

Low Income Families (LIF) statistics were produced by the Department of Health and Social Security for the last time in 1988 and based on the *Family Expenditure Survey*. LIF showed the numbers of people living on a low income – below 140 per cent of supplementary benefit. The Social Security Committee has commissioned the Institute for Fiscal Studies to continue publishing this series. CPAG argues that one possible poverty line is the income support/ supplementary benefit level. LIF uses: income based on the *Benefit Assessment Unit* (see above) rather than **household** income, as used in HBAI. The LIF uses **current** income (as is used in HBAI) and includes figures for Great Britain and the UK as a whole. Income is defined as: net earnings after tax, national insurance and super-annuation; gross profit from self-employment; all social security benefits *excluding* housing benefit; maintenance; investment income;

and some income in kind, such as luncheon vouchers, less tax and national insurance paid direct. The statistics show incomes after housing costs. Housing costs are defined as: rent and rate (net of rebates), water rates, mortgage interest, maintenance costs, etc, less housing benefit. LIF also uses different equivalence scales from HBAI (*see* equivalence scales).

Low pay – defined by the Council of Europe as 68 per cent of full-time mean earnings. In 1994 this was £221.50 a week, or £5.88 an hour.

Poverty definitions – CPAG uses two possible definitions of poverty: the numbers living on or below income support/supplementary benefit and the numbers living below 50 per cent of average income after housing costs.

Quintile group – successive fifths of all households arranged by income from bottom to top.

Single payments were grants for one-off needs such as cookers, beds and furniture, which provided extra help for people living on supplementary benefit. They were replaced by the discretionary social fund in April 1988 as part of the 1986 Social Security Act (*see* social fund).

Social fund replaced the single payments scheme in the Social Security Act 1986 (*see* single payments). The first part of the social fund was implemented in 1987 and provides grants for cold weather, maternity and funeral needs. It is governed by regulations and there is a legal right of appeal. The second part of the social fund was implemented in 1988; this mainly provided interest-free loans and has a small budget for community care grants to prevent people going into institutional care or to help them when they leave such care. Loans are repayable directly from income support at rates of 15 per cent in most cases (though it can be lower). This part of the social fund is discretionary and cash-limited and there is no right to an independent appeal, only to a review.

Social Security Act 1986 was the outcome of the 'Fowler Reviews' set up to examine the options for the major reform of the social security system. The Act brought in a new structure of social security that was fully implemented in April 1988. Income support replaced supplementary benefit, the social fund replaced single payments, family credit replaced family income supplement, and housing benefit was reduced.

Social Security Committee is a House of Commons Select Committee composed of MPs from all parties. Its responsibility is to monitor issues related to social security.

Supplementary benefit was paid to people who were not in full-time work and met certain conditions. It was replaced by income support in 1988 as part of the Social Security Act 1986. Supplementary benefit/income support is used by CPAG as one possible poverty line.

Unemployment Unit is an independent body which campaigns around, and does research into, unemployment and training.

Wages Councils, known as Trade Boards, were first set up in 1909. Trade Boards determine minimum rates of pay and conditions, backed up by the force of law, in certain low-paying industries such as retailing, hairdressing, laundries and clothing. The Councils were made up of employers, trade unions and independent members. Their powers were weakened in 1986 and abolished in August 1993 under the Trade Union Reform and Employment Rights Act.

Sources: DSS, *Households below Average Income: a statistical analysis, 1979-1992/93*, HMSO, 1995; Social Security Committee, *Low Income Statistics: Low Income Families 1989-1992*, HMSO, 1995; J Hills, *Changing Tax: the tax system and how to change it*, CPAG Ltd, 1989.

a secure future?

CHILD
POVERTY
ACTION
GROUP

Social security and the family in a changing world

LISA HARKER

Employment patterns and family structures have changed radically in the 50 years since the social security system was introduced. *A secure future?* examines who is losing out under this system and explores how social security could be remodelled to address the changed needs of the 1990s and beyond.

A secure future? looks at a range of different models of social security and judges them against criteria that include the ability to support new and changing patterns of work and family life. It is the first publication to assess a wide range of options in such a systematic way.

48 pages   0 946744 79 3   February 1996   £5.95

Send a cheque/PO for £5.95 (incl p&p) to
CPAG Ltd, 1–5 Bath Street, London EC1V 9PY.

And write for details of CPAG membership: Policy members receive publications such as *A secure future?* and *Poverty: the facts* automatically as part of an annual subscription.